WORLD'S FASTEST COFFIN ON WATER

The first-ever biography of Ken Warby

BILL TUCKEY

Published by:

Bas Publishing
ABN 30 106 181 542
PO Box 2052
Seaford Vic 3198
Tel/Fax: (03) 5988 3597
Web: www.baspublishing.com.au
Email: mail@baspublishing.com.au

The National Library of Australia Cataloguing-in-Publication entry

Author: Tuckey, Bill.

Title: World's fastest coffin on water : the first-ever biography of Ken Warby / Bill Tuckey.

ISBN: 9781921496066 (pbk.)

Subjects: Warby, Ken.
Spirit of Australia (Boat)
Speed record holders--Australia--Biography.
Motorboats--Speed records.
Motorboat racing.
World records--Australia.

Dewey Number: 797.14

Design & Layout: Ben Graham

For Toni McRae and Rob McCauley,
whose unswerving belief in the big bloke
led directly to the writing of this book

About the Author

Here we have a departure from the norm for author Bill Tuckey, widely known as one of the most respected motoring journalists in Australia. He has written 26 books, mainly on motoring and motor sport, the first in 1965. His most recent is "On Solid Ground", the history of 90 years of the Victorian Automobile Chamber of Commerce and the Australian motor industry and trade.

Before that came "Australians And Their Cars" and "The Sound And The Fury". His bets-known book is "The Rise and Fall of Peter Brock", published in 1987 and in 1987-88 was for several months on the natational paperback best-seller list.

Tuckey started in journalism as a copy boy on the Sydney Daily Telegraph newspaper, and worked on the Mount Isa Mail and Darwin's Northern Territory News before being head-hunted to the Adelaide News – then Rupert Murdoch's only newspaper. Then followed stints on the Sydney Morning Herald and Brisbane Courier-Mail, before becoming editor of Wheels magazine in 1963.

During his five years there he created the world's first multi-car comparison tests and inaugurated the Car Of The Year award, the world's longest-running such trophy.

In 1967-68 he was host presenter of Channel Ten's "Road Show", Australia's first television motoring program, which ran for 26 weeks. After a stint freelancing, he joined Australian Consolidated Press as a managing editor, alongside Ita Buttrose and Trevor Kennedy.

Returning to freelancing, he was motoring editor from the inaugural issue in 1981 of Business Review Weekly, a contract he held until 2002. From 1985 to 1990 he hosted breakfast and drive current affairs programs, first on Melbourne radio 3DB and then 3AW.

His many awards include the Royal Insurance Road Safety Journalism Award, the 1985 "Pater" broadcast arts and sciences award as best Australasian radio newcomer, the inaugural Dunlop "Motoring Journalist of the Year" award in 1985, in 1991 the CAMS Motor Sport Journalism award, and in 1993 was the first to be named to the Dunlop motoring journalism honour roll.

Tuckey has written, co-produced and fronted a number of automotive films and documentaries for television and cinema.

World Water Speed Record History

Until 1927 the record was unofficial because there was no recognised world body. The records were essentially plucked from those of organised power boat races. The first known record was set, incredibly, back in 1874, when on April 14, at Cheswick Reach in Britain, one Felix Haig piloted "Sir Arthur Cotton" to the heady velocity of 24.61 mph (39.5 km/h). Remember, this was long before the first world land speed record, set in 1898 by Count Chasseloup-Laubat at 62.8 km/h in his battery-powered "Jeantaud" electric car.

Until 1911 the records were set in succession by steam-powered, propeller-driven boats, like Nathaniel Herreshoff's "Stiletto" (1885, 26.2 mph/42.15 km/h), William Cogswell's "Feiseen" (1893, 31.6/50.8), Charles Parsons' "Turbinia" (1897, 39.1/62.91) and Charles Flint's "Arrow" (1903, 45.06/72.50).

The first major design changes came in 1908, when telephone inventor Alexander Graham Bell began running experiments with power boats. The first record set with what slightly relates to today's craft was Frederick Casey's 70.86 mph (114.04 km/h) in Bell's HD-4 hydrofoil on Bras d'Or Lake in Nova Scotia.

The official record rules were established in 1928, and from 1930 expanded to stipulate that a boat had to make two runs of over a timed kilometre course in opposite directions, the record an average of both runs. The official ratifying body is the Union International Motonautique.

OFFICIAL RECORDS

- December 4, 1928, Revier Canal, Detroit, Michigan, USA: George Wood (USA) "Miss America 7" – 92.84 mph/149.3 km/h
- March 25, 1929, Indian Creek, Miami, Florida, USA: Gar Wood (USA) "Miss America 7" – 93.12 mph/149.8 km/h
- June 13, 1930, Lake Windermere, England: Sir Henry Segrave (GB) "Miss England 2" – 98.76 mph/158.9 km/h
- March 20, 1931, Indian River, Florida, USA: Gar Wood (USA) "Miss America 9" – 102.25 mph/164.52 km/h
- April 2, 1931, Parana River, Argentina: Kaye Don (GB) "Miss England 2" – 103.49 mph/166.51 km/h

- July 9, 1931, Lake Garda, Italy: Kaye Don (GB) "Miss England 2" – 110.22 mph/177.34 km/h
- February 8, 1932, Indian River, Florida, USA: Gar Wood (USA) "Miss America 9" – 111.72 mph/179.75 km/h
- July 16, 1932, Loch Lomond, Scotland: Kaye Don (GB) "Miss England 3" – 117.43 mph/188.94 km/h
- July 16, 1932, Loch Lomond, Scotland: Kaye Don (GB) "Miss England 3" – 119.81 mph/191.16 km/h
- September 20, 1932, St Clair River, Detroit, Michigan, USA: Gar Wood (USA) "Miss America 10" – 124.86 mph/200.89 km/h
- September 1, 1937, Lake Maggiore, Italy: Sir Malcolm Campbell (GB) "Bluebird K3" – 126.33 mph/203.26 km/h
- September 2, 1937, Lake Maggiore, Italy: Sir Malcolm Campbell (GB) "Bluebird 3" – 129.56 mph/208.46 km/h
- September 17, 1938, Lake Hallwyl, Switzerland: Sir Malcolm Campbell (GB) "Bluebird K3" – 130.93 mph/210.6 km/h
- August 19, 1939, Coniston Water, England: Sir Malcolm Campbell (GB) "Bluebird K4" - 141.74 mph/228.05 km/h
- June 26, 1950, Lake Washington, USA: Stanley Sayres (USA) "Slo-Mo-Shun 4" – 160.32 mph/257.95 km/h

- July 7, 1952, Lake Washington, USA: Stanley Sayres (USA) "Slo-Mo-Shun 4" – 178.49 mph/287.19 km/h
- July 23, 1955, Lake Ullswater, England: Donald Campbell (GB) "Bluebird K7" – 202.32 mph/325.53 km/h
- November 16, 1955, Lake Mead, Nevada, USA: Donald Campbell (GB) "Bluebird K7" – 216.23 mph/347.91 km/h
- September 20, 1956, Coniston Water, England: Donald Campbell (GB) "Bluebird K7" – 225.63 mph/363.03 km/h
- November 7, 1957, Coniston Water, England: Donald Campbell (GB) "Bluebird K7" – 239.07 mph/384.66 km/h
- November 10, 1958, Coniston Water, England: Donald Campbell (UK) "Bluebird K7" – 248.62 mph/400.03 km/h
- May 14, 1959, Coniston Water, England: Donald Campbell (GB) "Bluebird K7" - 260.35 mph/418.90 km/h
- December 31, 1964, Lake Dumbleyung, Australia: Donald Campbell (GB) "Bluebird K7" – 276.33 mph/444.61 km/h
- June 30, 1967, Lake Guntersville, Alabama, USA: Lee Taylor (USA) "Hustler" – 285.21 mph/458.90 km/h

- November 20, 1977, Blowering Dam, Australia: Ken Warby (Australia) "Spirit of Australia" – 288.18 mph/463.68 km/h
- October 8, 1978, Blowering Dam, Australia: Ken Warby (Australia) "Spirit of Australia" - 317.60 mph/511.01 km/h

Foreword

He was quite mad, of course. Everyone knew that. A journalist who met him for the first time in 1965 says now: “He was just another speedboat driver, maybe a little bit more approachable." Said one of the people from Shell marketing, one of his sponsors: “He’s a showoff. He loves that sort of life. He loves attention.”

Just before midday on November 20, 1977, on a long, dark, echoing lake created by man’s desire for a dam to provide irrigation, lined by clay walls and reeds and chick-chucking red-bill swamp hens and a gypsy caravan of tents and trailers and little heaps of dead ashes and crushed beer cans and discarded Kodak packs, the private lunatic sat like a Mogadonned mouse in the jet-fighter cockpit as the boat he built under the cotton-easter trees in the backyard of his Sydney home blammed through the corrugations still left on the water from a ski boat an hour before, turning the surface into a cold tin roof. At the end, as they towed the Spirit Of Australia to where his grey-haired mother was sobbing on the edge of the lake, he had set the new world water speed record at 288.17 mph (463km/h).

In that instant he became a member of the world's most exclusive club. Today, it is even more exclusive, for he is the only member. Kenneth Peter Warby, now 69, is the only person alive to have held that record — which he still holds at 317.60mph (511.01km/h). All the others are dead — all 11 of them....John Cobb, Donald Campbell, Lee Taylor, Craig Arfons.....Said Bob Henderson, leader of the official timing crew for the first record: "For a few seconds that guy laid his life on the line. Everybody before who had been up to that point never got any further. It's like the sound barrier was. It was the unknown — nobody knew what was going to happen. It took a lot of guts......"

In April, 1980, the Spirit Of Australia was retired, eventually to find a home in Sydney's new Maritime Museum. The boat Warby had designed on a kitchen table and built himself, raising money by painting miniature pictures on timber and bark in every little shopping centre and agricultural show in every tiny tinpot town in Australia for three years, his wife Jan working as a draughtsman's tracer to keep food in the house, had mocked the mockers. There were civic receptions and sportsmen's awards, a valediction in Federal Parliament, and the award of the MBE in the 1978 Queen's Birthday Honours. Yet Warby was cynical about the plaudits. "The boat is open now for the highest bidder. It doesn't matter if it's Idi Amin wanting it for his flagship for the Ugandan Navy. I've done my bit for God and Country and got yawned at. Now I can go out and make a buck." It was easy to draw the parallel with fellow Australian battler Alan Jones, who lived in Europe in sleazy tenements and sold used campervans for a living because he couldn't get a single dollar from Australian companies to help him towards the goal he finally achieved — that of Formula One World Champion in 1980.

Warby likewise got little or no support from Australian industry and commercial sponsors, and only back-door help from the Royal Australian Air Force. "If I'd lived in America I would certainly have had a lot more money than I had after the first run. I was offered $100,000 after that to run the Spirit in America renamed after a US product but I refused." And yet, after the Australian Government paid to send him to the US on a six-months' tour of 25 cities with the boat as a sort of roving sports ambassador, he turned his back on Australia. Warby moved to the States, started building jet drag cars and eventually monster quarter-mile trucks, and his country forgot him. Perhaps his only material link was that he started building small-capacity concrete mixers, an Australian innovation little known in America.

Warby became a bitter man. "Here they stand with their hands over their hearts to sing the Star-Spangled Banner; in Australia they don't even know the words of their national anthem."

And yet it had taken 23 years of brutal struggle to take Warby from his first boat Hellcat, capable of only 25mph, to the final record of 317.60mph (511.01km/h), 23 years of character-building and grinding money-grubbing to where Kenneth Peter Warby. MBE. Sportsman Of The Year, Outstanding Boatman Of The Year, holder of the

King George V Trophy, became the first Australian ever to hold a world speed record for land, sea or air. Importantly, he didn't do it alone, and he recognises that, despite his lingering sorrow about the way his country has largely ignored him. At last count it took 162 people, all unpaid, to put the Spirit into the water for that glorious final weekend; among them were a scientist and a senior military intelligence officer, a top car race driver, and the man who nine years later would stage the world's first long-distance race for solar-powered electric cars. It cost him his marriage, and almost certainly weakened the heart condition of his mother Evelyn, who would die three years after the day the triumphant Spirit was towed back to shore and she, then 69, cried weeping: "You'll finish now? No more?" Warby put his arm around her, saying: "Come on, old Sal; we'll talk about it later," and then into the thrusting microphones: "She said that about my first boat — and it would do only 25mph. How are you, you bloody old scene-stealer?" But it hadn't really been his first boat; that was a rocket-powered model of Donald Campbell's Bluebird he had built at 13 years old to fire across a swimming pool in the working-class city of Newcastle where he was born.

The Spectre of Death

The first world water speed record was set in December, 1928. It was the era of giants of speed, of Boy's Own Annual heroic deeds, of huge engines, of vast bowls of race tracks, of crazed midget cars on every fairground in America, of aircraft-engined behemoths spraying rooster-tails of wet sand a mile along as they thundered down the beaches, tyres being slashed by seashells, the monstrous 400 horsepower Liberty aero-engined Babs buried in the Welsh Pendine Sands where its huge drive chain broke at 180mph (290km/h) and took off Parry Thomas' head. He and Malcolm Campbell and Henry Segrave and Kenelm Lee Guiness (who gave his name to KLG spark plugs) were all chasing the Wakefield trophy, inaugurated in 1928 by Lord Wakefield of Castrol fame, for the fastest man on earth — a title that dated all the way back to 1898, when Count Chasseloup-Laubat reached 62.8km/h in his electric battery-powered Jeantaud.

On that day in June, 1929, when Sir Henry Segrave climbed into the cockpit of his boat Miss England II, he was aiming to be the first man to hit 100mph on water — Campbell held the land speed record at 206.95mph at the time. However, Segrave failed, and when he was killed a year later, on June 13, in his second attempt, the Americans took over, just as the Brits were monopolising the land speed record. In 1932 Garfield Wood hit 124.9mph (201km/h) on the Detroit River, and Malcolm Campbell's Bluebird upped the record again and again to 141.2mph (225 km/h) until by 1952 it stood to the credit of American Stanley Sayres, at 178.4mph (287km/h).

It was time the British got the record back. The man to do the job was John Cobb, whose elegaic 2500hp Napier-Railton in 1947 had elevated the world land speed record to an incredible 394.19mph (634.25km/h). And the jet engine, a child of war, would replace the piston-engined monsters used on land and water before. In September, 1952, Cobb went through the timing traps on his first run in his jet boat Crusader at 206mph (331.45km/h) — seconds before Crusader took off and turned itself into flotsam and jetsam and Cobb into a statistic.

Haunted by the heroic land speed record conquests of his haughty and aristocratic father, Donald Campbell built a boat using a Gnat jet fighter engine with basic thrust of 3800 pounds — the same output Warby would use two decades later without the afterburner on his Westinghouse J34. Complex, insecure, superstitious, but commercially far from naive, Campbell called his boat Bluebird after his father's succession of LSR cars, and in July, 1955, quietened at least some of the rattling chains of his father's ghost when he set the two-way average over the measured mile of 202.3mph (325.5km/h).

For the next decade, while massaging British industry for the money to build the Bluebird car to attack the LSR, Campbell kept raising the water record. His friend and chief mechanic on both projects was the puckish Leo Villa, who had worked with Sir Malcolm and who would figure largely in Ken Warby's life later. In 1964 Campbell brought Villa, his Norris-Proteus-powered car and the boat to Australia, where he had identified as an LSR site the great salt lake, Lake Eyre, which sees water perhaps once every 20 years, when pelicans and fish appear as if by magic, 1500km from the sea. At Lake Dumbleyung, in Western Australia, with his lucky teddy bear mascot Mister Whoppitt in the cockpit, Campbell kicked the water record up again, to 276.33mph (441.61km/h). And after months of waiting for the right weather, with a vast backup of the Australian Army and sponsors fretting in London about their funds, Campbell overcame his fears and took the Proteus-Bluebird across the two-way mile over the mud-streaked Lake Eyre salt for a new LSR of 403.10mph (648.5km/h). His record would last for less than a year; the American drag racing Summers brothers team with their Goldenrod, with an engine at each wheel, would take it to 409.68mph (659.27km/h). It stands to this day as the world land speed record for a wheel-driven vehicle; everything since has been by pure jets.

Campbell knew nothing but record-breaking, and probably because the commercial world had grown weary from the tales of his prevarication and stalling at Lake Eyre

— one story was that he was being paid per day by major sponsor BP Petroleum, so the interminable waits — he found it hard to raise money. He decided to take the water speed record over 300mph as a great gesture, a sort of Grand Guignol, a statement that would put to rest the stories that he was not the brave man his father was. Leo Villa, of whom more later, was utterly against the project. Tracing his mechanical training from a 14-year-old with Isotta-Fraschini (he never did an apprenticeship) Villa, born a Cockney within the sound of Bow Bells in 1899, knew Cobb's boat had been destroyed by too-high impact loadings. He had test-driven Campbell's boat ("when I first sat in it I hoped it wouldn't start, but it did") and repeatedly warned Campbell the aerodynamics would start lifting its nose over 250mph (426 km/h)..

In 1967, on the gloomy, eerie Coniston Water in the England Lake District, Campbell whistled through the mile at an average 478.17km/h — but before he lifted-off it had topped 328mph (527.7 km/h). This gave Campbell the heart and the balls; but on his return run the blue boat took off on the vertical plane and set off on a violent cartwheel for almost a kilometre. They found Mister Whoppitt, but never Campbell. Six months later Lee Taylor Junior, of Downey, California, took the record back to the US when his hydroplane Hustler averaged 285.213mph (458.3km/h) on Lake Guntersville in Alabama.

This was the record that Ken Warby faced 10 years later, on Sunday, November 20, 1977, at Blowering Dam. But when he snatched it, and then a year later kicked it up further by becoming the first to beat both the 300mph and 500km/h barriers on water, Lee Taylor refused to believe it was possible, and came back at him. On November 13, 1980, on Lake Tahoe, in a jet-powered boat that Warby two weeks before had told Taylor would kill him, the American drowned, still strapped into the cockpit of what was left after his hydroplane took off. Taylor had refused to hand over the King George V world water speed trophy to Ken Warby for 18 months after Warby took it.

His death made Ken Warby the only member of the world's most exclusive club.....

The Cold Hands of Coniston

It is fair to say that Warby is obsessed by Donald Campbell. It is possibly because the spectre of the long-dead Campbell frustrates and annoys him on many levels. He was always irritated that the Australian Government and companies well-represented in Australia — Dunlop and BP among them — gave so much support to Campbell's almost-comic opera world land speed record epic on Lake Eyre, yet threw Warby out of their offices a few years later when he came cap-in-hand pleading for sponsorship money. He was annoyed because he saw Campbell as a wimp, where Warby is totally self-assured, eternally in control, able carefully to calculate the last degree of risk, willing to seek out and take expert advice. When, well after Campbell's death. he exchanged a number of audio tapes with Leo Villa on the progress of the design of the Spirit Of Australia, he became more and more contemptuous of what he saw as Campbell's foolhardiness. Ken Warby thought mindless courage was the province of fools, and few things annoyed him more than idiot journalists asking him about his "death wish."

Years later he would say he achieved his records on what Campbell had used for beer money. "Campbell had a habit in Australia of charging everything to Bluebird, but Bluebird never had a bloody bank account! There were a lot of unpaid bills in this country relating to Campbell - one beach-front hotel in Adelaide was owed a thousand quid by Campbell for booze. The whole Campbell episode was involved in horseshit. He really went through millions and millions.

"I think originally his father had the money and the ability and the style to carry it off. Donald didn't have the money but had a lot of his father's camp followers and tried to live in the style of his father. There was a lot of media-grabbing bullshit. One wonders how much of Campbell was for real, but I admire the guy for his guts." Here again we find Warby quick to blame the media.

But still Campbell fascinated him. Through months and months of taping and subsequent interviews for this book, he would refer obliquely to an eerie experience at Coniston Water, where Campbell died, but would cut it off with his typical jerk of the beard and "Let's get onto more important things." He finally put it on tape, with the warning that he had never told anybody —anybody — about what happened that night in the bedroom of the hotel in which Donald Campbell slept before he died, and that I might find it disturbing. And then something very strange happened.

It was near the end of the tape when he got on to the subject of Coniston. "It was a beautiful clear day. There was one cloud in the sky. We stopped the boat where Bluebird was, and we stopped right under the cloud shadow. A coincidence. I threw two wreaths on the water, and suddenly the cloud moved away and we were in bright sunshine. Just a coincidence. I'd met Leo Villa at his Surrey home — he was one of those unsung heroes who make guys like me look easy — but I'd never met Donald Campbell. But I felt very close to him. Had he been alive there would have been a lot we could have discussed that no-one else could have understood, like why we do it. I would have liked to have gone to the lake and sat under a tree and thrown a few rocks into the water and just talked to him about what happened after we threw the wreaths, but then......"

Warby had talked before to a few people about what he called "a way-out experience" that he couldn't explain or understand. He regretted not having written it down at the time, and put it into a sealed envelope in a bank vault. The tape went on: "If what happened can be believed — and I went through it — I don't understand the reason for it or how it works or anything else, but I know what I experienced in that room, or if there was a message to be gained from it." On the tape there was a pause. He thought about it. "When I die it will be a coincidence; we'll meet up or I'll just rot to death with cancer or something, but I don't think I've got any right to say where or when, or commit suicide." But what, I asked, was the something strange that happened at Coniston?

And then the tape jammed.

I tried everything, even dismantling the player. But every time I re-started, the tape minced itself more, until there was a spewing of sad thin brown worms clogging the orifices. I rang Warby in Cincinatti in the US and told him. There was a long pause. "Jesus Christ", he breathed. "I can't talk about that again."

But he did, back in Australia in January, 1991, after a long time, sitting across the desk from me.

Now, Warby, you see, is a hard man. He was a Newcastle boy, a steelworks boy, and his steelworks father knew the Great Depression and he did it hard, and his grandfather before him. Warby never had any illusions; he never thought anyone, let alone the world, owed him a living. Least of all was he a romantic — he crucified his first marriage and family on the altar of his obsession to become exactly what he became. But as he talked about Coniston the great craggy face softened and the eyes lost their glitter and the strong jaw concealed by the great raw beard trembled from time to time. When he said "I'm sorry", and his eyes glistened with tears, we stopped for a little while.

He went on the pilgrimage to the black Coniston Water in 1979, with his London friend Kevin Desmond, after Lee Taylor Jr had killed himself and Ken Warby's marriage was ruined and his life had become empty because after what he had done with Spirit where else was there to go for the loneliest man on earth? Desmond had told Warby about Campbell's psychic experiences, that during one of the runs, either in the boat or the car, he claimed to have seen his father's face in the windscreen. After that Campbell regularly used to consult a medium to try and make contact with his father. Warby says Desmond tried to persuade him to do the same; "I told him it was just a lot of hogwash." Desmond had apparently found Campbell's sister, who had agreed to go through the seance.

"I stayed at Kevin's house in Olive Road, North London. I had always wanted to go to Coniston, and now the feeling was very strong. Kevin said he would take me there, because he knew the people, and I was an honorary member of the K7 club, which was Bluebird's boat number. Speedo's Australian public relations boss David Thomas was on holidays in London with his wife and we all went to book in to the Sun Hotel at Coniston. We went out to throw the wreaths." Warby says that all the way out to the centre of the lake he kept thinking of the little Bluebird model boat and the Jetex 50 engine he put on it back in Newcastle so many years ago. But typically, while remembering that, he couldn't recall the wording on the wreaths. "I think it said: 'Take care of the skipper.' That was what Villa always called Campbell.

They stayed that night in the hotel where the Campbell crew was based for the Coniston attempt. "We were all bullshitting around and playing darts and a lot of locals came in to meet us and all that."

Although he didn't know it, Warby was sharing with Desmond the room in which Campbell had slept the night before he died and his body vanished beneath the black lake.

"I was laying in my bed.....I heard a hell of a scream....it must have been the ugly early hours of the morning. I sat up. The bed head was against the wall, but somebody — something — came behind me and put cold, wet hands over my eyes and pushed me back down on the bed. Then the voice said: 'It's OK. Three will die before the record's broken once.'"

What sort of voice was it?

"It was a very cool, British voice. A calming voice."

What happened then?

"Then the hands went away."

Warby said nothing to his friends. Driving back to London, Kevin Desmond said to him: "Something happened to you last night. You're very strange." He had heard nothing during the night, although he was asleep in the other bed. But he then told Warby something he hadn't mentioned before — that Warby had been sleeping in the bed Campbell had used.

Warby had been telling the press he was going to build another record boat. He had built a model of Spirit Of Australia II, a boat to do 600km/h, a boat to cost $250,000. Soon after Lee Taylor was killed in what the US press called his "$3 million coffin" Warby put his model on the shelf. Early in 1987 Craig Arfons, nephew of Art Arfons who had set the world LSR three times with his jet-powered "Green Monster", the last at 928.2km/h in 1965, took an F5 fighter General Electric J85 jet out of his drag truck and stuck it in a Deaver hull, stretched a couple of metres to fit the engine behind the cockpit. "He knew I used a wedge shape, but he never saw it", said Warby later. "A drag boat has a wedge to get it up on the plane, but all this thing was going to do was fly. I used Arfons' workshop for a couple of months to work on jet cars and I pleaded with him to take it to Marietta in Georgia and put it into the wind tunnel the NASCAR cars use. But he thought he knew it all. It was obvious he was going to get positive lift and he would kill himself. Maybe he realised the real truth at 268mph (430 km/h) when it took off."

The cock had crowed twice, with thrice to come, and the Warby record was still intact.

Hard Yakka

Newcastle is aptly named. Like its older namesake Newcastle-on-Tyne in the British Midlands, its heart is that of a gritty, tough, grey, self-reliant industrial city. After dawn the suburban parks are still trodden by men walking greyhounds, the working man's hobby, and there are racing pigeon lofts atop the long terrace house rows in the inner suburbs. It was typical that when several suburbs were ruined and a dozen people killed by a major earthquake on December 28, 1989, Newcastle largely looked after its own. It was also typical that in 1997, a few weeks after being devastated by the news that the city's main steelworks was to close, its young Rugby League team, the Steelers, would win the Grand Final by scoring with just seconds to go to full time.

Dominated by its giant steelworks and shipyards, the harbour a mouth to a sullen brown river that leads inland to the brighter sunlit uplands of the Hunter Valley, where great grape vines grow and craft and antique shops wait for the tourist and the convention business, Australia's sixth largest city, 171km north of Sydney, was discovered in 1797 by a Lieutenant Shortland. He was searching for convicts escaped from the 10-year-old first settlement, and instead found coal, which was to be the base for the area's mining and steel blast furnaces for the next 180 years. It says something that Newcastle's sister city is Ube in Japan, a grim, loveless prison of a town, a restored wartime Zero fighter the rooftop emblem at its airport.

But a tough steel town always produces achievers, because they struggle to escape. One of the world's greatest billiards-snooker players of the post-war era, Eddie Charlton, is a Novocastrian; Craig Johnston became the first Australian to reach the pinnacle of England's fierce soccer pile, including an FA Cup final.

The Warbys were all Newcastle, and the Bydders before them. The Warbys were originally from Wales; Ken is a sixth generation Australian and the family legend is that one Ben Warby was the last white settler seen by explorer Hamilton Hume and sailor William Hovell on their epic but argument-ridden trek to Australia's southernmost coast in 1824. It is a sweet irony of history that a cairn marks the site of Ben Warby's house about three kilometres north of the statue that signifies for the tourists the place of the famous song, "Nine Miles From Gundagai."

(The original poem ran thus....

"'Twas getting dark, the team got bogged, the axle snapped in two.

I lost my matches and my pipe, oh, what was I to do.

The rain came on, 'twas bitter cold, and hungry too was I,
And the dog shat in the tuckerbox, nine miles from Gundagai...."

But Victorian-era sensibilities censored that to "the dog sat on the tuckerbox".) A further irony is that the Ben Warby cairn is about 100km, as the crow flies, from where his descendant would later become the world's fastest man on water.

Ken Warby's grandfather James died at 96. He walked down the front path and out through the gate to the ambulance, pausing to pat his wife Elizabeth on the head and said: "You've been a great girl for me all my life." Said Ken: "His clock just ran down. A week after he died she just gave up and died too. She was 89, and didn't want to live any more." His grandfather had been born at Maitland, now about an hour's drive west of Newcastle, in 1858. He was that most admired of Australian bush heroes, a consummate horseman, horse breaker and drover. He was part of a legendary drive of 1000 head of cattle from central Queensland 3000 miles south to Deniliquin, and he broke horses for the Army during World War I. His wife, born Elizabeth Ann Osmond near Dungog, broke horses too, only sidesaddle; "it was unladylike to ride astride."

Warby says his grandfather talked about knowing the bushranger Captain Thunderbolt, and fighting-off marauding Aborigines during his droves. He used to show them a big Colt revolver he carried when he was part of the "posse" sent to hunt down Aboriginal murderer Jimmy

Governor and his clan around the turn of the century. "He used to tell the story about how he climbed in one window of a house as Governor went out the other." The whole tragic episode was later re-created in Australian author Thomas Keneally's book "The Chant Of Jimmy Blacksmith", and the movie made from it.

James and Elizabeth Warby were married on October 26, 1884, and had 13 children, some of them born in wagons and drays on the droving trips. One of them was Ken's father, Neville Stanislaus Warby, named after an old bush nanny called Nurse Stanislaus, herself named after a Polish king. He was born in 1905 at a place called Largs, near Maitland, today maybe an hour's drive west of Newcastle, then just a big bush town, famous as the birthplace of Les Darcy, whom folklore has it was the greatest fighter Australia has ever produced, a man who fled to America to escape conscription for World War I and who died there soon after of an infection from rotting teeth.

Neville Stanislaus Warby was born a typical Australian bush kid. His father James farmed when the years were kind, generally as a share farmer for some rich squatter, taking what was allowed to him off the acres, always the rough end of the pineapple. Neville remembered first a big property called Brindley Park, near Merewether, where his father was a horse breaker, worked sheep, drove the big ancient narrow-tyred wool trucks. As a horseman he was more than what Australians then called a "rouseabout", but he didn't have his own property, nor the status of the black-singleted shearers who would move from station to station in the season, earning big money, drinking away their cheques when the rains came down.

When Neville was maybe eight years old the family moved back to Largs, to a dairy farm at a dot on the map called Iona, his father now not able to do the hard yakka of droving and breaking, instead become what was called a "cow cocky", milking 100 dairy cows twice a day, victims of a 365-day-a-year schedule to get the milk and cream separated and into the churns on the sled for the big Clydesdale to tug up to the front gate, maybe a kilometre away, for the milk truck to collect and take down to the big factories in the towns. The cream they kept went into home-made butter and cakes and puddings; the milk to the pigs and the poddy calves being fattened for sale, the little calves butting their heads into the bucket and sucking hard-gummed on the children's winter fingers reddened by chilblains.

Like all farm kids, school was a place to be, bare-footed and freckled, only until the law allowed you to leave. At 14 Neville Warby went out to his first job at one pound a week and all found — good money in 1919 but up at 5am and back from the paddocks at eight o'clock — on a farm called Phoenix Park. After 12 months he was sick of the slavery and handing over half his money to his mother, and headed for "the big smoke" — Newcastle.

There he got a labourer's job with BHP — Broken Hill Proprietary, the huge company that had even then become a legend in Australian mining and industrial development. As most of the unskilled labourers did then, he found himself in the blazing red Hades of the steel rolling mills, working his way up through the gangs until he became a foreman of the construction squad that would build the new enormous blast furnaces, modern pyramids erected by the sweat of swarms of men manhandling barrow-loads of concrete up sloping ramps. But then the Great Depression hit, and Neville Warby was laid off. Luckily he was friendly with a girl who worked in what was called the BHP Job Search Office, and he worked there through the second half of the 1930s as well as driving a truck (called a "lorry" in those days) for a friend whose company made fibrous plaster sheets for builders.

In 1932 he met Evelyn Dora Swanson. Five years younger than Neville Warby, she worked in an office and he met her at his sister's place in a Newcastle suburb called Adamstown. She was the daughter of a Baptist minister from Maitland, born in Toronto, then a small town not far south of Newcastle. But there had been a nasty, sad divorce, and as often happened in those times — particularly where a man of the cloth was involved — she was handed-over to an accommodating and religious family to raise. Ken's sister Ida would say in 1984: "We were never allowed to find out grandmother had left home when her youngest was six weeks old. We saw this old lady in black at a funeral in Stockton but we were told never to talk to her. It was rather a strange background, because I felt sorry for kids who were better off than us. We had to keep the family tail up because of our past life. Mother was always very concerned about what other people thought."

Mother, Evelyn Swanson, the one who would later weep by the edge of Blowering Dam, was handed over to the

Bydders, he the grandson of one Charles A. Bydder, born in 1826 in Chatham in England. Here began the strange thread linking him to the Ken Warby who would later become an engineer and a boatman; Charles A. Bydder was apprenticed at Woolwich in 1842 and by 1847 was a third-class engineer on the Royal Navy's HMS "Fishguard"; he served on a number of ships to rise to the rank of Fleet Engineer — about equivalent to a Major in Army rank. Ken Warby remembers grandfather Bydder as an inventor, a photographer in the time when the technology was glass slides, a man "with lots of patents". His brothers and sisters recall better the woman they called "Ma Bydder", who brought-up their mother Evelyn and had a lot of influence on the four children of Neville Warby and his wife Evelyn — whom he always called "Polly" or "Tot." They remember her as a "very cultured lady"; certainly, she raised Evelyn to a strict set of values which she in turn imposed on her husband and her children.

Later, as a schoolkid, Ken Warby would blast away all Grandpa Bydder's priceless glass negatives with his air rifle, and smash-up his great old wooden camera to make a model of a boat......

Tale of a Tired Heart

New Lambton is a suburb about eight kilometres from the centre of Newcastle. It was middle class for the Warbys; by 1990 it had become yuppieville. This family then would have been offended if you had described them as poor, because they really were very representative of what was then "lower middle class." Today - particularly in Australia, where years of unremitting social engineering from a succession of Federal and State governments has made a virtue of forced mediocrity, of taxing small business to underwrite extravagant social welfare visions, of political correctness of expression - this would be actionable as discrimination. But in those days people either recognised or decided the meniscus of their class, and rose to it as well as they could.

The house at New Lambton was large and Edwardian in style on a big double-sized block, built in timber, with four bedrooms and a corrugated iron roof. Somehow - Ken Warby still isn't sure how because nobody talked about it, but one suspects Grandpa Bydder had helped, as parents often did in those days when young 'uns found it hard to save a deposit with only one partner working - Neville and Evelyn had managed to buy it around 1939 from a butcher called Payne, who bred show jumpers and was the Mayor of New Lambton. There was fine proud cedar panelling with stained glass windows, and a big walk-in pantry, a large main room with a fireplace and a vast solid cedar sideboard and an old chaise-longue, in the kitchen a large gas stove with a wash copper set in concrete, two concrete tubs and a tall cupboard where the pots and pans were kept.

The big kitchen was the centre of the universe. Nobody used the front door; there were double French doors down the side, opening onto the big main room. There was an air-raid shelter in the backyard; Neville Warby had been exempted from war service but was a member of the special squad with the responsibility of demolishing the entire BHP steelworks if the Japanese followed up the few shells they fired into Newcastle from a submarine.

There were big gaps between the five children they had. Neville arrived in 1936, Ida 1939, Ken 1940, Rob 1942 and Andrew 1944. The last three were born at New Lambton; Evelyn had a midwife for all of them. Ken Warby's closest childhood friend, Ross Morgan, remembers her as extraordinarily kind-hearted, even though she was never well. "She spent all her life looking after the kids, and looked after Ida's when she worked. Neville was a simple, quiet guy. None of us was flash, just Newcastle battlers. But we could go to the Warby place any time. It was always a happy place - you could just walk in. I felt a lot of love and affection in that house."

But their mother Evelyn was never well. Says Ken Warby now: "She was a sick woman all her life. It was nothing for Dad to come home and find Mum passed out on the floor. She was bed-ridden a lot." Sister Ida, quiet, beautifully spoken, articulate, says Ken's mother tended to try and wrap him in cotton wool. It was family rote that he suffered from something called a tired heart. "She used to make a thing about him having a small passage in his throat, and how he tended to choke, and how he almost died when he swallowed a coin. It wasn't until his teens that he went off and did all the mad things.

"Mum made the decisions, but she used to have blackouts. Sometimes the neighbours would smell the gas and come in and rescue her. My father was a great disappointment. Money was always extremely tight. Ken never had clothes but he never cared about clothes anyway; he mostly went to school barefoot. I married a man I thought was like my father and I found out that that's not what you should necessarily do. Mum made the decisions and he went along with it. My mother had an extremely strong will. She held the family together, so it started disintegrating the day she died."

Ken Warby confirms this: "When Ida was 12 the doctors suspected mother had a brain tumour and sent her to St Vincent's in Sydney. She saw people there she thought were like vegetables and refused to have an operation. Maybe it was a blood clot....anyway, she kept having blackouts....my dad sometimes had to stop her swallowing her tongue in a fit.....sometimes found her wandering miles away. She couldn't cope with the heat but she wore black at weddings and going shopping. We kids took it in turns to take a day off school each week to look after Mum."

But Evelyn still ran the Warby household with an iron rule. Warby says she was fanatical about a clean house, and would vacuum it every day. "I can remember her sitting up in bed telling me how to cook a bread-and-butter pudding for the family. Whoever was home that day had to do the cooking and all the orders came from the front bedroom." Warby says his father Neville never raised his voice to mother or children. Apparently a man willing to sacrifice for peace, he deferred to her in every confrontation. "It used to be a standing joke with us kids.....Mum would come storming out and say 'Your father said you've got to do this!' and we'd say, hell, what rot, father never said that, it was her idea."

His father Neville took refuge in his greyhounds, as so many Australian men did in that period. His brother Percy, Ken Warby's uncle, used to own and train trotting horses, so that provided an escape as well. Father Neville said of Ken years later: "He wasn't all that interested in school and not that interested in sport either. He was supposed to have a tired heart, whatever that was; you know, he wasn't real energetic, if you know what I mean".

When Warby's father said that in an interview in the mid-1980s he was disgusted with his famous son, whom he hadn't seen for a year. "To tell the truth I would care....it don't matter if I don't see him again. If he can't come and see the old man....he's been in Newcastle and Sydney and can't even ring up. We'd go down and watch him (during the record attempts) and he'd have all these other blokes around him....he got all the glory. I wouldn't be one of those who rushed up to him and say congratulations, Ken. What's the use — don't even worry about it".

But Warby remembers his schooling differently. He had to repeat fifth class in primary school because most weeks he had taken a day off to look after his mother. In a long series of interviews with New Zealand writer Toni McRae in the early 1980s he said: "I had a lot of good teachers who were prepared to spend extra time with Ken Warby. We spent a lot of time with this Methodist guy who used to present history well. I wasn't impressed with church - so many hypocrites......people telling how you should abide by the 10 commandments on Sunday and spend the other six days breaking them". How do you feel about God? "I believe there's a God. I've always felt that but I don't believe I've got to be a Sunday go-kneeling type. He knows what you're doing. You know in your head what you've done. To me religion is more a state of mind and loving your fellow man. I sit back and reflect within myself about what's going on and communicate that way".

Warby says his mother was his biggest influence, laying down the rules of manners, doing the right thing, accepting responsibility, supporting the family. "I used to run messages for a Mrs Needham across the road. She was a herbalist, and I got three shillings for five afternoons a week. Then I got a real job, although I was still at school. This was as a messenger boy for Neil Smith the chemist, and that was a really big shop because I earned 30 shillings a week for two hours every afternoon and three hours on Saturday morning. You see, our parents couldn't afford to give any of us pocket money." Later, for one shilling and sixpence per hour, Warby would go from the pharmacy to turn-up nuts and bolts on a small lathe in the engineering workshop of a man called Bruce Jarvie, who expanded later into a large engineering business.

Warby is blessed with a photographic memory. Even today he can visualise the blackboard he faced in Broadmeadows primary school. In the Intermediate Certificate - which in those days meant you were halfway through secondary education and aged 14 or 15, old enough to leave school but with two years to go before sitting for the Leaving (matriculation) Certificate that would take you to university - he passed with four A-levels and two B-levels and moved to Newcastle Technical High School for those two years. "I wanted to be a pilot, then I was going to be a manual arts teacher, so I took metalwork and woodwork and technical drawing for the Leaving Certificate. Jeez, I remember: The teacher was called Mister Fitness. I topped the state in woodwork. I was determined to do better than my brothers and sisters. I was the only one to get the Leaving and become a Queen's Scout and a Scoutmaster".

He says the Scouts became something of a second family; "they taught me teamwork, resourcefulness, coolness under pressure....we used to walk for days with just a pack and a compass through the Barrington Tops jungles. If you've snapped a rope and you're halfway down a cliff and you're not sure how you're going to get out of it it's no good sitting there screaming your lungs out".

His closest boyhood friend, since they were both 11, Ross Morgan, was an only child who lived just around the corner and went to the same infant's and primary schools, Warby one month younger, and Morgan destined to be best man at his first marriage. When Morgan's father Cec (his mother's name, unusually, was Alfrida) was in the Middle East and Borneo during World War Two the pair would invade the traditional Australian bloke's sanctuary of "the shed". Morgan says now: "We'd build things. Dad came back from the war and found all his nails and screws gone and the tools wrecked". Morgan, who became an industrial architect, says Warby is one of the rare people who can make anything with his hands. "He's incredible. He's just got enormous natural mechanical understanding and knowhow."

He says Ken was always something of a black sheep. "Neville (four years older) did all the right things, did his apprenticeship as a fitter and turner, worked his way up with BHP, got married, had kids, didn't build boats and race all over the place." Robert, two years younger than Ken, also went to work for BHP but had a dreadful accident. He stumbled into a 1200-degree molten metal pool from the blast furnace and it ran into his boots and ruined his leg; the doctors wanted to amputate it but he said no, and they saved it.

Says Morgan: "Ken spent a lot of time at our place. His Mum was very kind-hearted and looked after the kids, but his father was a simple guy. None of us was flash - after all, it was a battler's town. My father drove a truck and there was only one car parked in the whole street and that was a 1926

Essex. We never owned a car". He says Warby was nicknamed "Tum" and "Doorknobs", but can't explain why - "except he likes his tucker and doesn't exercise. We used to play cricket in the front yard of the Warby house but he'd sit on the fruit box and play a cheap guitar. He was mad-keen on country singer Slim Dusty". Warby has never lost that: On all his long dark kilometres driving through Australia the Slim Dusty tapes always filled the cabin - and still did all the way across America. He has 23 eight-track cassette tapes of the Australian country music legend.

He played Australian Rules football and competed with the Newcastle Swimming Club, but he was never much better than average. He was more interested in building model aircraft, and somewhere in the process carved out of balsa-wood a model of Sir Malcolm Campbell's Bluebird boat. At 16 he was at a Boy Scout camp on the edge of Croudace Bay on Lake Macquarie, south of Newcastle, when he came across a 13-foot racing speedboat on the sand. The impact was profound. "It looked so simple to me", he said later. "I knew there and then that I wanted a boat just like that. I sat down and designed what I thought a speedboat should be like". What he built in the backyard was a plywood-and-maple boat, 10 feet long, with a 1934 Ford Prefect four-cylinder engine.

It took him almost a year, turning-up parts of it on a lathe at technical college, borrowing 25 pounds (today about $200) from his father Neville to buy the old engine. "I couldn't afford a trailer for it so I made up a wooden box trailer on some old springs. I towed it out to Croudace Bay, but it would get up on the plane and then just flop down".

Even then the design was radical; the bottom was concave, not convex. Ross Morgan: “It was like nothing you’ve ever seen. The thing almost turned a back somersault every time he put the power on, and it was always breaking down. But it didn’t stop him. Whatever else he wanted to do then, he wanted to be the world’s fastest man on water”.

Ken Warby triumphant atop the Spirit after he lifted the record to where it still stands – 511.01 km/h. This was his second major sponsorship, Speedo.

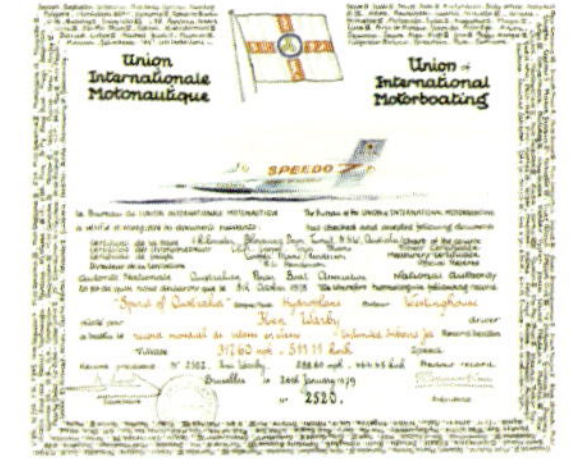

Union Internationale Motonautique

Union of International Motorboating

SPEEDO

2520.

The official world water speed record certificate, issued by the Union of International Motor Boating. Eleven good men and true have died for it.

Roger Climpson hosts Warby on "This Is Your Life" in 1979, with wife Jan alongside and sons Michael (left) and Peter (in glasses) behind them.

With Australian Prime Minister, Malcolm Fraser, in 1979. "I've done my bit for God and Country and got yawned at. Now I can go out and make a buck".

Sir Malcolm Campbell, who set world speed records on land and water, thus leaving an impossible legacy for his son Donald. Sir Malcolm died in bed.

Amazingly, the "puckish" Leo Villa was involved with Sir Malcolm and later Donald Campbell, and finally, Warby. He was chief mechanic on Bluebird.

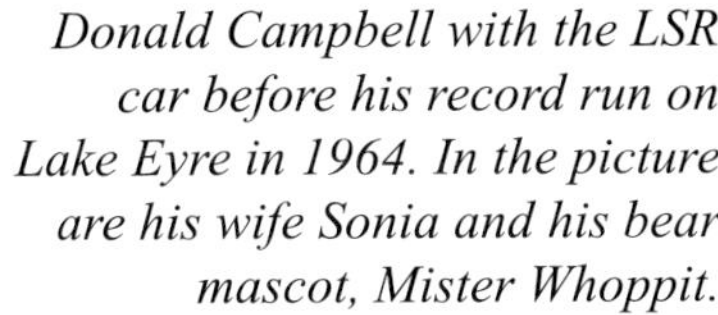

Donald Campbell with the LSR car before his record run on Lake Eyre in 1964. In the picture are his wife Sonia and his bear mascot, Mister Whoppit.

While at Lake Eyre Campbell took the Bluebird boat to lake Dumbleyung and cranked the water speed record to 441.61 km/h – Warby's target.

Coniston Water in the English Lake District, the site of a number of record attempts. It is a favourite British holiday and boating destination.

The small four-star Sun Hotel at Coniston, where Campbell's Bluebird crew stayed and where Warby had his spine-chilling encounter in Campbell's bed.

There is no doubt Ken Warby was fascinated by Donald Campbell from his youth. This was one of the last photographs taken of the doomed Britisher.

In 1979 Warby went on a pilgrimage to Coniston Water, to place a wreath, with the inscription "Take care of the skipper" to honour Donald Campbell.

His new world record behind him, but his marriage ruined, Ken Warby contemplates Coniston in 1979. With him in the boat was Kevin Desmond.

Warby's grandmother, Elizabeth. Born in Dungog (NSW) she had 13 children, some born on droving trips. She died at 89, a week after her husband.

Ken Warby's grandfather James, who lived to 96, was a legendary bushman who took part in the hunt for Aboriginal mass murderer Jimmy Governor.

Ken Warby's father, Neville Stanislaus Warby, with his beloved motorcycle and sidecar. He had a hard early life in the bush before joining BHP.

The obligatory embarrassing shot of Ken Warby as a baby on a spread quilt. He was born in 1940 at New Lambton, with the help of a midwife.

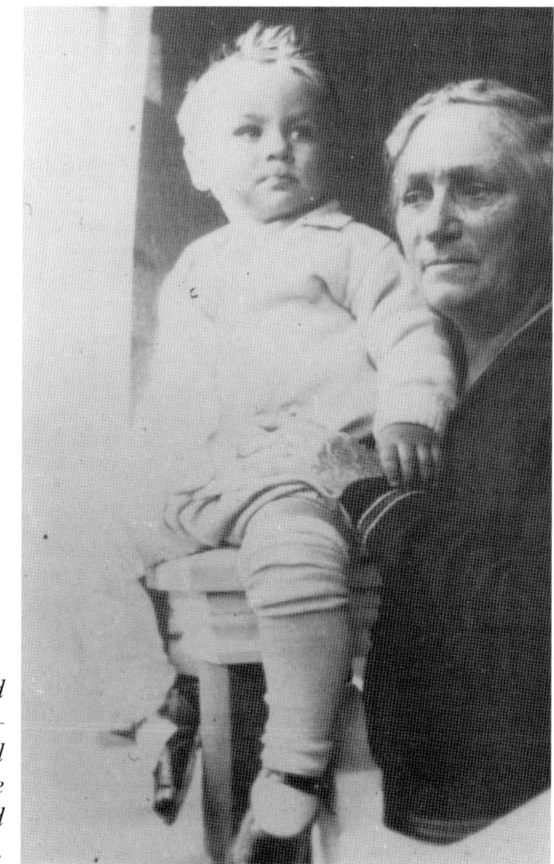

The Warby children called her "Ma Bydder" – Warby's maternal grandmother, here holding the two-year-old sixth-generation Ken.

The chubby three-year-old Warby, all spic-and-span in bow tie and carefully-parted (and doubtless Brylcreemed) hair, for a family studio portrait.

An obviously ill-at-ease Ken Warby with school friend Judy Mort before a "miniature debutante dance" at New Lambton, some time in 1950.

New Lambton school, Class 5A, 1950. KW is third from left in rear row. His nicknames included "Tub" and "Doorknobs"; he was never keen on sport.

Warby in horned buffalo hat at a 1957 Scout camp at Lake Macquarie in 1957. It was here he saw his first speedboat, which inspired him to build his own.

Warby's first boat, "Hellcat" was a flop, and his second, called "Rosslyn V", which he changed to "Rebel", was no better, although it looked the part .

"A beaut little runabout" was how Warby described "Falcon". The first boat he built himself, it ran a six-cylinder Dodge engine, later a Mercury V8.

In 1963 the 23-year-old Warby married Jan, a Catholic-raised girl he met at a dance at the Empire Palace in Hunter Street, Newcastle. It would last 15 years.

A rare shot of the three brothers together – for Ken's 1963 wedding. L to R Neville, Robert and Ken, the youngest, and regarded as the "black sheep".

The unbeatable "Monte Cristo" at Goolwa (SA). This boat brought him his first sponsorship - albeit small – from STP and Dulux, but it bored him.

Waiting for a TV interview with NBN3, Warby and his first race team, the Royal Rebels, and runabout class "Black Mac" with Shelby-Cobra engine.

Of Testosterone and Nautical Phalluses

Warby had painted the name "Pablo" on that first boat but changed it to "Hellcat", doubtless to try and shame it into going faster. But it never had enough power. His father Neville: "Then he said to me one day, if I can sell this boat Dad, can I buy another one? I said what sort do you want to buy? And he said a 15-footer, a second-hand old thing. I said, yeah, that would be all right. I helped him out with some money".

Warby stole from the American *Popular Mechanics* magazines in the libraries drawings of the Campbell and Segrave record-breaking boats and made models to fire across a pond at New Lambton. When Hellcat didn't work according to his theories, which included a concave hull shape instead of traditional convex, he became what the motor sport inner circle calls a "pit pest". He haunted the Newcastle Royal Motor Yacht Club boat racers, particularly a car dealer called Eric Henshaw, who had the fastest boat around, called Joker, with a big-block

Chevrolet V8. "I'd bum around his yard in the afternoon and learn what I could. Most of the guys in boat racing then were used car dealers. I think the finance companies owned most of the boats".

Warby bought his second boat in 1958, a 10-footer called "Roslyn V", but he changed the name to "Rebel". It was another disaster, so he and a friend called Jimmy Dick together built what Warby today describes as "a beaut little runabout" called "Falcon", with a six-cylinder side-valve Dodge engine that could take it to 40 mph, later replaced by a V8 Ford Mercury. Then, as things go in the testosterone-driven world of teenage speed kings, Jimmy Dick got married, joined the police force for security, and his next appearance with Warby was as his groomsman. Warby had also come to some sort of terms with reality, signing-on with BHP as an apprentice mechanical engineer, a place opened-up for him only through his father Neville, starting on drawings and designs in the ominously-named Coke Ovens Office. Falcon wasn't a bad gadget; with Dick riding shotgun it set a new record for the 255-cubic-inch capacity on the RMYC's championship course at Toronto, south of Newcastle. He had had his first taste of real speed driving a hydroplane called "Raider", which he rebuilt for its owner in his Newcastle backyard in 1965 and which could top 100 mph (160 km/h) when it wasn't breaking bits.

His life was changed by a boat called, romantically, "Monte Cristo". It had been around for a while, called "L'il Goldfinger" in the strange cult that men have for naming their nautical phalluses, owned by an up-country farmer called Mike Crawley. It was then a crude but effective 15-foot Ford V8-engined racing skiff. "He could never get it going properly so he asked me to have a look at it. I pulled the tops off all the carburettors and found the needles bent, so I straightened that out and jumped in the boat and gave everyone hell. Mike asked me to drive it in the 1967 state titles at Cabarita (in Sydney) and we won what was called the Whisky Cup". His father Neville was less subtle. "It was owned by this chap from Tamworth and it was fast but he wasn't game to drive it more than half pace. Ken was only 17 and Mum used to worry a bit. but not too much. She used to come out Sundays to watch him. It never entered me head that he would go on - it was just that it was instead of cricket or football with this tired heart. He used to read a lot of books and maps about boats. I hadn't a clue where he got the information. Horse racing was my sport".

Warby bought Monte Cristo just before Christmas in 1967, the green-and-gold-over-black wooden-planked boat destined never to be beaten in its racing class. With it he won the Whisky Cup two more years in succession as well as the NSW 266-cubic-inch state title and finished second in the nationals. In the fairly narrow and little-publicised world of powerboat racing, he was becoming mildly famous. Brother Rob, two years younger, the only other one in the family interested in speed, was less than impressed. Speedway bikes and cars were his thing, but he would say later: "We used to laugh at Ken - he couldn't ride a motor bike - and his boats but when he broke the world record at Blowering we stopped laughing." Even at that time Rob was saying: "He'll carry on with boats until one day one kills him, I reckon. That or a car, one or the other". Then when several years later Warby was driving the world's fastest jet drag car Rob would say: "Well, that'll kill him, I reckon". His father Neville would disagree: "I have that much confidence in him". Rob: "Boats go only so fast and then they take off. Sooner or later something's going to happen. I've got confidence in me brother too, but one can only go so fast". He could see no sense in going "whoosh" (as he put it) in a straight line in drag cars. "Speedway takes more skill. It's the most skilfullest driver, I always told him."

At that stage one of his best mates was Ray Lynch, who raced a hydroplane called "Lynchee". But a bad car crash broke his pelvis and he gave away racing boats to help Warby prepare his. "He arrived with this boat in the yard (it was Monte Cristo) and said, 'In a week's time we're going after the national titles'. I don't know if I taught him much about boats. I tried to calm him a bit. He's a man with no fear, with the greatest driving ability, no nerves at all. But teaching Ken anything.....I don't know. I don't think so. But I always had a gut feeling he was destined for greatness. He was fanatical about doing everything right. For me to have a motor functioning as best as I could do it on a shoestring - we never had any money - and to have a driver who would drive right to the limit, you know........" and he trailed off into thought...

When Warby was starting to test Spirit of Australia he wanted Ray Lynch to ride with him. "He'd bought two-way radios and he said: 'You know hydroplanes and you know the water and you can tell me when to back off'. I would have backed off miles before Ken did and I said no, I'm sorry. That's when I wiped my hands of it. I would have been calling him and saying, hey, back off boy....I just didn't want to put myself in that position. I wouldn't go to Blowering. I was scared for him. I don't think Ken will die. I just told him not to try and advance the record any more until someone's beaten it".

In 1967, after eight years with BHP, Warby set up a small sales company, called J.K. Trading, which handled things as diverse as road brooms, lubricants and printing machinery. "I was getting tired of the red iron ore and the heat and the dust, breathing it all the time. Still, it was marvellous how many foreign orders were built in BHP workshops that got my earlier boats going — I remember building rudders and cavitation plates, steering pulleys, all sorts of bits and pieces". His sales activities led to him into Worthington Australia as a sales officer, dealing mostly with BHP in supplying materials and equipment to its shipbuilding yards, sugar mills, pipeworks and acid manufacturing companies. Monte Cristo by now had brought him his first major sponsorship, with the American oil company STP, renowned for its involvement in the Indianapolis 500, and he picked up some money from the Dulux paint people, but it was still a battle. He and another mate, Allan MacIntosh, formed the Royal Rebels Racing Team, with sponsorship from the Newcastle Mercury outboard motor dealers, comprising Monte Cristo in the skiff class and MacIntosh's runabout class "Black Mac" sharing the one 266-inch Shelby-Cobra engine, swapping it over between races, even in the national titles.

But Warby was getting bored with Monte Cristo. "It was too easy. If you put it in the water and it floated and the engine started you won. The hull was built by Lewis Brothers in Sydney and what it did was read the water".

When he was 23 years old, he married Jan, on January 22, 1963. Twenty years later, just after the divorce, Warby would say: "We never should have got married. I want to live to a ripe old age and there's a lot of sins I want to commit yet".

He Called Her the Fuehrer

Jan came from a strict Catholic family, but her parents did the unforgiveable in those days by separating. In Australia then, this was social disgrace, to be concealed at any cost. Mostly the children were packed-off to church boarding schools up-country, which was where the Sydney-born Jan went, into the care of the Black St Joseph's, frequent flourishers of the split cane, Mass every morning at six o'clock, seven days a week and twice on Sundays, the nuns concealed from their Communion repast by a screen, any contact with boys punished by a postponement of your Child of Mary status, warnings against patent leather shoes because boys could see in them reflections of your undergarments.

She and Ken met at a dance at the Empire Palace in Hunter Street, Newcastle — he doesn't remember the year. "We chose each other, but we were never totally tuned in on each other's wavelength", he would say years later. "I used to call her The Fuehrer. It was just a fun thing when I started with her, but only a joke. I was racing boats when I met her and it's not as though I changed my life - I just extended on what I was already doing."

His mate Ross Morgan can't remember how Jan came on the scene. "She was always in the background". Said his brother Rob: "She didn't mix real well. She was very quiet, shy or something. She never went anywhere much with him". Ray Lynch's wife Daphne would say later: "I didn't know Jan all that well, but I'm sure she loved him. She always went to the yacht club for special occasions or a big race day and the presentation balls. She never really put Ken down. I would say she backed him, but was a little bit frightened about what he was doing. She never confided in me any problems about the marriage".

Warby, tall, handsome, talkative, persuasive, charismatic, with a huge appetite for sex that was fed somewhat by boat race groupies, was never averse to what Australian men then used to call "a bit on the side". He was advantaged in this by the fact that his shy new wife didn't much like the company he kept - the boat racers, the used car people, the club officials. "What sorts of people they were I don't know", he would say later, disarmingly (although he would start having his own bitter problems with the jealous racing fraternity the moment he became famous); "they were basically everyday people, a few wheeler-dealers, but basically good people. She preferred not to mix with the race boat crowd.

"She was very unforgiving. I had a friend when I was only going out with her and he got a little drunk and misbehaved in front of her and he was written-off her books for ever and a day. In the end she went at her own pace. I didn't force her to do anything. If she didn't want to go anywhere she didn't,and I attended most of the boating functions on my own. It would probably have been more beneficial to the marriage had she stood by my side".

It is a multi-faceted profile, remembering that Jan endured and somehow adjusted to the vicissitudes of the massive Warby achievement drive. Asked to define him, Ross Morgan says: "He's probably an extrovert — he gets an idea in his head and nothing stops him. He's a very self-reliant sort of person, prepared to give up jobs to stay involved in racing". Ken's sister Ida, articulate as always, almost (and certainly without knowing) defined the difference between the Protestant work ethic and the Catholic guilt burden: "I think Jan's a nice person but she just couldn't cope. Some people cope with problems, some don't.. I have a different outlook on life to Jan; I don't care how tight money is or how long you work in the job. I don't think it's any excuse to have a house looking like it did. She wasn't a good hostess but Ken never criticised her". Warby certainly had a major fight with his mother about the marriage, and didn't speak to her for four years afterwards. "It took those four years to slow Mum down. I went back more for Dad's benefit than Mum's".

Given the inestimable value of 20/20 hindsight, it is now obvious that Warby was then (and probably still is) a selfish man by today's politically-correct standards. But 30 years ago the right word was "dedicated", and as such, he was. For the first few years of their marriage they lived quite well on both wages while he raced his boats, but he wanted more space for the boat that was creating a madness in his mind and after landing a job in Sydney in November, 1972, he rented a house in the northern suburb of Gordon, and moved Jan there with their three children.

It was then that he started spending money on the dream - Ross Morgan says Jan virtually "kept him most of the time", which Warby even today denies. "I think I was fair to Jan. I think there was a lot of money put towards the boat we could probably have put on other things, but money was made from the boat. They may have gone through a couple of hard years but everyone had clothes and a roof over their heads and they weren't hard done-by".

But did he spend enough time with his family? "I think I did. I was never one for sitting beside a river and having a little family picnic. I don't think the kids were treated like royalty, but then again they really didn't do without much". He admits now the marriage would not have lasted even if he hadn't been building a boat to go for the world record. He describes it as a gradual disintegration over a very long time: "Jan found it difficult to make friends but when she did, they were friends for life. We sort of drifted apart. I became much more of a loner, and she turned within herself. There was no big fight or anything like that".

The difficulty one must have with all this is with trying to identify the origin of Warby's innate selfishness - for there is no doubt that while we can cloak it in the smoke and mirrors of words like bravado and ego and derring-do and macho he never for a moment deviated from the notion that he would be the world's fastest man on water. There is the conflict between his mother's inner strength and his father's shield of submissiveness to her. It might also be Ken Warby's resentment of the fact he was the middle child with a heart murmur, that his father always referred to the younger son Rob as his "golden boy", or the way his mother may have used her health problems to command obedience from her children, like demanding they lose one day a week from school to look after her, or even maybe staging her black fits.....

Asked about some of these things, what comes through from Warby is one essential truth; it is that he never lies to himself. "I am what I am, and I do what I do, and maybe I'm just different", is the only way he ever explained it. Anyway, it all went wrong. The marriage ended some months after in 1983 Warby decided to go and drive jet dragsters in the US. But back in 1969 in Newcastle, Kenneth Peter Warby had started drawing the first sketches of the insane boat in his head. It was to become the Spirit Of Australia.....

At the Stoned Crow

If anyone ever had a doubt about Ken Warby's road to Damascus it would be dismissed by the knowledge now that in 1969, when he was sketching his first rough ideas for a world record-breaking boat, he bought two RAAF surplus ex-Neptune bomber Westinghouse J34 jet engines from the Federal Government for $100 each. He and Ray Lynch drove from Newcastle west to the big provincial city of Dubbo to collect them. They sat in a couple of Newcastle backyards until Warby moved to Sydney. There in 1972 he bought a third engine, this time for $65, from the government stores in the Sydney suburb of Regent's Park — "just for spares", he said at the time. As it turned out, that was the engine that broke the world record.

The boating writer who first recognised the demon in Warby was Graeme Andrews, now a bearded Sydney tug boat skipper. They met for the first time at the Royal Motor Yacht Club in Toronto in late 1965. "He was just another speedboat driver", Andrews would say 20 years later. "But he was more approachable and you could get answers that weren't monosyllabic. He wasn't talking about world records then; his main ambition was to win class races".

He says Warby first mentioned the world speed record program to him in 1970 or 1971. "There are two kinds of people — those who say they're going to do something and those who do. When I first saw the drawings, I thought, well, he's going to kill himself, but that's his right". In the November, 1972 issue of *Seacraft* magazine he broke the first story. Headed "I'll do 200 mph on water! — Warby", it showed a sketch of what the story called a "28-foot plywood jet-powered monster", plus photographs of the inverted, part-finished hull, an engine, Donald Campbell at speed in Bluebird on Coniston just before he crashed, and Lee Taylor's boat "Harvey's Hustler", which in 1967 in Alabama had left the world record at 285.313 mph, with a Westinghouse J46 jet.

Warby designed the boat on his kitchen table. "I'd got to the stage where I was tired of going around in circles and I'd seen photos of Taylor breaking world records and decided to build a drag hydroplane to do it. There was just one page of pencil detailed drawings. I did them late in 1970 sitting in the Pymble (Sydney) lounge room of my friend John Biddlecombe. I was sitting there fiddling with a pencil and I drew the boat. There were no secrets in it. People looked for things that weren't there. It was always going to be simple because I didn't want to go to aluminium or exotic carbon-fibre or fibreglass. There's a certain amount of flex in timber than can be useful, aluminium is difficult to work and fibreglass must have a perfect mould." Just like that. There, in several sentences, were dismissed many of the theories and computer modelling of the world's best fluid dynamicists.

What he designed was actually a conventional hydroplane, which skims along the top of the water, planing on three tiny surfaces — the two sponsons, like little skis, up front, and on the propellor at the back. "Like a three-legged table, it's more stable than a four-legged one". The hull was to be made of plywood over a frame of light, strong aircraft-quality spruce with four main "stringers" of straight-grained yacht racing quality oregon stiffened with an epoxy fibreglass material called Dymel. "I went to a place called Whittakers to get some 32-foot lengths of that oregon and they had one huge block they'd been keeping for special occasions — they cut it up for me". Warby says he had read what he could find on boat design, which wasn't a lot, but he knew what he needed — a boat similar to Lee Taylor's but better-balanced and designed to run on rough water. He did no stress calculations. It was "pure eyeball engineering from building and driving boats, even down to the thicknesses of the timbers".

A film maker Rob McCauley, later to produce the definite video of the record attempts, remembers meeting Warby for the first time at Sydney's Port Hacking Motor Boat Club to film a TV segment on safety in offshore racing. "Afterwards we had a drink and the next time I saw Ken was at the Stoned Crow wine bar in Crows Nest. Ken said: 'Look Mac, bring your camera over to my place next weekend. I'm going to start laying the keel for the fastest boat in the world'. I thought I'd never heard so much bullshit in all my life, so I completely ignored it. Months later I met him in the same bar and he issued the same invitation — but he never mentioned jet engines. I said: 'Yeah Ken, I'll do that', and I thought, who does this bloke think he is? He's going to outdo Campbell and Cobb and Segrave — all the names I knew as a kid?"

McCauley went overseas for more than a year and came back to a contract with the national broadcaster, the ABC, to do a pilot boating program. "I had an old phone number for Ken as a Makita power tool salesman, and they gave me his home phone number. I went out to his Concord home. It was very dingy, very ordinary and in the backyard was this monster of a hull with this old jet engine mounted on it. Christ, I'd never seen anything in my life like it, and here's old Warby with a grin all over his face. He was very excited and enthusiastic, and he was showing me everything and saying that's what I told you about a year ago and you never came down and filmed it". But McCauley's ABC producer at the time wouldn't have a bar of the story, so McCauley started "borrowing" ABC film to shoot the progress work in secret.

McCauley still shakes his head over how such a boat was ever built in the chaos in the rented house. "Jan fed the kids and went to work and paid the bills and Ken, well, if he had any affection for her he never showed it to me. She was like a housekeeper — it was never a real family atmosphere. The back verandah where Ken worked and stored bits and pieces for the boat was a bloody mess, untidy as all hell. I thought he was selfish. He had tunnel vision. He totally gave up work to put all his energies and money to make that boat the best in the world. I remember him saying: 'Does she care? I don't know. But I'm going to do it anyway'. In the backyard he couldn't even turn the hull over. If he wanted to do that he would have to take it up to the park and get whoever was there to help him". McCauley continually marvelled at Warby's ability to get people to do all sorts of things to contribute to his dream.

About this time Warby was starting to fall victim to his enthusiasm and his mouth. He was claiming the boat would do 300 mph (480km/h), and the usual press misreporting of what was then a little-reported sport didn't help — one Newcastle *Sun* story had it powered by a jet engine from a Hercules bomber (the Hercules C130 is a turbo-prop cargo aircraft in basic form). Another had him attempting the world record on Lake Munmorah, near Newcastle, a pond by comparison with what would really be needed. By the end of 1973 photos were appearing of the boat on trailer and floating, but it hadn't been launched and Warby had done the publicity only to try and solve his main problem — lack of money. He had been out to the Richmond RAAF base west of Sydney and met jet engine technicians Peter Cox and Rex Crandall, who offered their time free to re-work the engine wiring and plumbing and run it up on a test pad. It was all back-door stuff, no public money involved, nudge-nudge, wink-wink, you know.

On June 2, 1974, driving a seven-year-old Ford Falcon, he trailered the half-finished Spirit south-west to a lake at Griffith, a big country town with a name writ large because of its association with the Italian Mafia, marijuana plantations and the controversial murder of anti-drugs campaigner Donald Mackay. With no rear engine cover,

Warby sitting in an open cockpit ahead of the jet intake, it was the first time the jet had been fired-up on water. "I just put the foot down and as the boat kept accelerating and as long as it felt good I kept going until we ran out of lake — it was a very short lake. I probably got to 150-160, maybe a bit higher". The Australian water speed record at the time was 163 mph (262.2 km/h), held since 1969 by one Tom Watts in a hydroplane named "Exciter", running an old Meteor fighter jet engine dating back to the early 1950s, crudely lashed to the hull with logging chains........eight years later he was killed trying the same engine in a drag truck.

Warby announced he would try for Watts' record at Lake Munmorah. But already some sections of the press were scorning it as "Warby's White Elephant". When three weeks after Griffith he hit a beer can at 152 mph (245km/h) and the boat started to sink, rescued from shallow water by 15 men with a tractor and the turbine blades damaged by ingesting water, the sceptics homed-in. Even when in September, two months later, he averaged 167 mph (268.7 km/h) with a top speed one way of 209 (336), to get the national record, they were sniping. Said Warby later: "It was pretty much the joke of the town....the boating media were having a field day. The boat wasn't finished, there was no engine cooling, and the Maritime Services Board refused to let me run until the registration numbers were made bigger and I had passed a noise meter test. Things started to get better after I got the Australian record but I still copped flak from various people".

Bob Henderson, former official of the Australian Powerboat Racing Association, wasn't one of the knockers. "He built his boats well, not like packing cases. There was no reason he couldn't succeed (breaking the world record) given the money, the time and experience. There was the worry, the fear he might kill himself....I'd seen a couple of guys killed. At Munmorah he lost it and some things were missing like the scoop at the rear of the hull and part of the wedge. I remember somebody yelling out 'he's gone'. It wasn't a matter of Ken building the boat and running it three or four times and breaking the world record. It went on for a long time, and there would be periods when the thing would never get in the water, could be 12 months or more, while he was working on a particular problem." The particular problem was mostly money, and it exposed Warby's irrational impatience with the drudgery of knocking on the doors of big corporations, but still produced a typically-idiosyncratic Warby solution. He became a painter.........

Fink, Doctors and Bark Painting

In May, 1975 Warby resigned his job as a sales manager for an import company. "A couple of friends, John and Eileen Bishop, were doing display work in shopping centres, such as the world's biggest jigsaw puzzle, the world's biggest crossword puzzle, stuff like that. John encouraged me into painting things people could afford in shopping centres, like five-dollar miniatures". He'd never painted before, let alone in oils, but found he had a natural talent for it, painting a landscape on bark or balsa in about five minutes.

He started in a corner of a shopping plaza in Woden Place in the national capital, Canberra, and was soon making far more than his job had been paying. So he began touring the country, shopping centres and caravan, car and boat shows, selling five-inch by four-inch (12.7x10.1cms) paintings for $5 each and painted maps of Australia on white masonite for $20 each. Then he got to the stage of trailering the boat along and doing the paintings alongside.

In the meantime he had met the wonderfully-named Professor Tom Fink, the man to whom Warby gives most credit (apart from himself) for Spirit. "I knew Lake Munmorah was too short. It had only about a mile run-in and a mile to stop and I was lifting-off halfway along the course. I knew I needed advice on aerodynamics and surfaces, particularly air scoops and maybe a tailplane. All there was, was this hull and engine and me sitting in front of it". He knew Fink, formerly a lecturer at the Imperial College in London, had done the aerodynamics on Campbell's Bluebird boat and one of his students, Ken Norris, actually designed Bluebird. Warby tracked him down at the University of NSW in Randwick in Sydney, where he was Dean of Engineering. "I did it a little bit arse-about-face. I got into his office and Tom said: 'This is great, but where's your wind tunnel model?', so I went home and built one. He later told me the first test figures were better than Bluebird's".

Professor Fink was born in Frankfurt, Germany, and his parents fled to Britain in the mid-1930s to escape the Nazi regime. He came to boats through an intense interest in aircraft and the use of wind tunnels for aerodynamics. "I hadn't heard of Ken until he walked into my office at the University of NSW. He said he had read about me in Campbell's book, I think.....he thought I might give him some advice on the next phase of development of his boat and I said something like, well, it's always interesting to meet somebody who intends to kill himself and he said something like, well, that's why I've come here - to avoid that".

Fink's student, Norris, had been put through an aeronautical engineering course by his two brothers, who then brought him into their Sussex consulting firm as a junior partner. Campbell gave them the job of designing his Bluebird boat and Norris said it must have a wind tunnel test. Fink: "It was done in a very British way. Ken Norris rang me to say that Donald Campbell was a client of theirs and would like to meet me and would I be available for lunch one day. I was still fairly junior and didn't know about British lunches. We arrived at Rules restaurant in the West End (of London) at 12.30 and finished about 4.30. Campbell said he wanted to break the world water speed record, which was then 178 mph and he talked about the bad luck previous contenders had had hitting logs in the Lakes District. He described graphically what a railway sleeper looks like floating vertically to within an inch or so below the surface. That all struck me as very odd.

"We decided to get hold of news footage from various attempts and look at it one frame at a time. This showed violent oscillations before breakup. We calculated stresses and the Norris brothers designed the sorts of stresses fighter aircraft then had, but couldn't use some aerodynamic aids because they were banned by the international boating control body. You couldn't have a tailplane, for instance, so that as the nose came up you would present more and more frontal aspect and thus produce the loop-the-loop phenomenon". The design team had to fit plates between the front sponsons to keep water out of the engine intakes, and these tended to exaggerate the lift. "I gave Donald a series of maximum speeds, above which he must not go. If it had stayed level, OK, but the slightest wave it would loop the loop. It finally did that at 320 mph (515km/h). But Ken's boat.....I've seen it go in what by Campbell's standards would have been extremely rough water".

Fink says he believed Campbell was mostly very afraid of what he was doing. But Warby was never any different, whether under stress or not. "I'm not trained to judge characters or describe them, but I think he tried to be a normal, solid citizen throughout this enterprise - kept it normal. I think Campbell wasn't a showman but felt he had to put on a show. Ken Warby is a showman but subdues it". When Campbell died Fink was in Australia. "When I heard he hadn't waited for the lake to settle down after his first run but came straight back, which broke all the rules everyone had ever given him, because of the instability of a boat running into your own wash is one way of getting the nose up and allowing the wind to push you up more.....On a truly smooth lake with no wind it wouldn't matter, but even then it's madness to run into your own wash.

"Many of us felt maybe Campbell was quite suicidal, or maybe something was going wrong with his new marriage. Campbell had a degree of fanaticism and that's quite dangerous really. During the trials there was all that water coming into the air intakes and he refused to take it easy so his chief mechanic, Leo Villa, had to put a wooden block - in fact I helped him put it there — under the accelerator pedal, unbeknownst to the driver. Now that's no way to do business, really".

Why did he decide to help Warby? "Because he asked me. If I thought he would have made a mess of it I wouldn't have. You don't want to be associated with obvious or even less than obvious failures, but he had a substantial history behind him. It was obvious from the start that he was prepared to listen". He said Warby had a "much above average" comprehension of what he was doing. He was surprised he built his own wind tunnel model, because normally that needed professional technicians, but Warby came back to him in a month with a near-perfect model. Wind tunnels are now common tools, but few know the Wright brothers built the first. Trying to decide what shape to make their wings, they hit on the bright idea of setting up a large propellor to blast air through a duct onto a model and measure the forces involved; today's wind tunnels use exactly the same principle on a far larger scale.

The tunnel tests at the University of NSW, run by the equally-wonderfully-named Dr Lawrence Doctors, a lecturer in mechanical engineering, told Fink the boat needed a tail-plane to take the weight off the rear wedge through a positive "angle of attack". Boat designers know that the faster you go, the more a rear wedge exerts forces on the water, so the laws of physics, which determine equal-opposite reactions, promote the tail-up nose-down attitude. But the faster you go the more the aerodynamic forces lift the nose, and the tail-plane is there to balance-out both.

By this time the Union of International Motor Boating had altered its rules to allow wings and fins. Warby would eventually have the tailplane built in aluminium by a Canberra aircraft component maker called Aerosmith, using second-hand wing tips from a Cessna 182. The air intake Fink also wanted became a glass-fibre Y-shaped duct bolting onto the front of the engine, there mainly to dispel the turbulence from the air flow. He said later: "I didn't have any apprehension that he would kill himself. I knew he wouldn't take too big a leap forward. The boat had behaved itself without a tailplane and with it would be better". Warby: "He's a very methodical, very precise man. He was very concerned that we wouldn't push the boat past the design limits. He had worked out that the top speed of Bluebird should be 250 and Campbell tried to do 300 and killed himself; the boat was never designed to do that". Dr Doctors was less sanguine; after a press conference in January, 1975, he was quoted as saying the tests indicated the boat would flip backwards if the bow lifted by only 0.4 of a degree. "At really high speed, without major changes, he is likely to kill himself".

Rob McCauley was there at a meeting after the tunnel tests and was amazed how Warby would argue and bandy theories with Professor Fink, one of the world's experts in fluid dynamics. "There was a particularly big argument because Ken said the boat needed a V-shaped wedge and Tom Fink disagreed. He said it wouldn't make any difference, but Warby said he'd do it anyway. We said goodbye and as we got into the car Ken said: 'Well, his books and slide rule might tell him one thing but my bum tells me the V-shape will make the boat ride better'. The next time I was out at his house he had this huge 10-foot long piece of oregon cut into a vee and it was going onto the boat". McCauley today still feels that was what gave Spirit its magic. "It doesn't mean all the experts were wrong - just that Ken's bum was more right".

But now came the problem of finding the water to run the Spirit of Australia towards these new-found design limits.

The Glorious Hero Media Manual

In late 1974, in Perth (WA) on business, Warby had checked-out Lake Dumbleyung, where 10 years earlier Campbell had run Bluebird. It was then thought to be the only stretch of water suitable, in a country the same size as the mainland US. But Warby knew what it would cost to move the boat, the support infrastructure and the media to such a remote place.

He had also opened his big yap to the media again. In December, 1974, he held a press conference to announce he would have a go at the world record the next year, probably at Lake Dumbleyung, even though at this stage the boat still didn't have a rear structure, tailfin or air vents — in fact, the engine still had to be moved a metre forward as Fink had demanded. Somebody should have told him to shut up, but he had no sponsors apart from Shell, so he thought this might be the best way to get attention. What it did, when he kept postponing his runups and trials, was to antagonise an already-sceptical media. But he was full of good quotes, like "Obviously I don't want to have the fastest coffin on water", and "The thought of death doesn't worry me though perhaps the possibilities of death are better than evens", and "I just want to gain the prestige for Australia" — all good 15-second sound grabs.

The press responded well, the Melbourne *Truth* newspaper of December 21 running with: "Ken Warby knows that a tiny ripple on a lake could see him torn limb from limb in a fraction of a second. He knows that the slightest breath of wind could spell a violent end to his life". The Sydney *Daily Telegraph* of January 16, 1975, in huge headlines yodelled: "A floating matchstick could spell disaster for Ken!"

At the big Aquatic Carnival weekend in the NSW mid-North Coast town of Taree at the end of January, Warby tweaked the half-cobbled Spirit through a couple of demonstration runs. By March he was saying the record attempt wouldn't be until December. At Lake Munmorah near Newcastle on July 26 he ran the boat for the first time with the engine moved forward. Then came one of those flukes that seemed to follow Warby through his life. Rob McCauley's film about Spirit went to air on the ABC and a week later he got a phone call from one Graham Thompson, president of the Tumut Progress Association. Tumut is a pretty town about four hours' drive south of Sydney, approached through long avenues of tall poplars, and Thompson wanted Warby to have a look at a dammed lake called Blowering. Lake Blowering hadn't existed when Campbell went to Dumbleyung, because it was one of the last lakes formed by the gigantic Snowy River Scheme, to this day the biggest civil engineering project ever mounted in Australia, revolutionising the way the southern half of this arid country is irrigated and giving employment and new hope to thousands of migrant workers from war-devastated Europe.

By this time McCauley had assumed the role of ex-officio public relations manager for Warby, so strong was his belief, writing endless submissions to potential sponsors, to little avail. Boating writer Graeme Andrews had introduced Warby to Shell marketing executive Cyril Arnold, thus gaining him his first real sponsor. “It was no big deal for me. Just as a journalist you get to meet a lot of people and you put them together to mutual advantage. I stayed close to Ken mainly because I could see the potential for good stories. I was never one of the knockers. Ken Warby is not the only one in the game I helped in many ways but he was the only one who's ever come back and said thank you”.

In mid-August, 1975, Warby, McCauley and Arnold flew down to Tumut in a brand-new Beechcraft Debonair piloted by David LeClair. McCauley popped a bottle of champagne at 8000 feet and half of it baptised the new plane; Warby had already told the pilot his boat was faster than this aircraft. To this point Cyril Arnold's sponsorship had been mainly in the form of free fuel, help with accommodation expenses and making typing and copying facilities available. He couldn't get Shell to tip in much more, and one feels he didn't really think the whole thing was that much of a big deal. When Warby gave the big thumbs-up to Blowering, the town of Tumut, population then about 7000, went mad, of course. The *Tumut & Adelong Times* predicted a spectator crowd of more than 15,000 for the record attempt, said Tumut motels had offered free accommodation to the Warby team, and that the police and emergency services were already preparing contingency plans.

On his second visit to the town a month later, Warby even named December 6 as a tentative date for the attempt — but the boat at this stage still hadn't been tested at any speed with all its new aerodynamic aids. Trumpeted the *Tumut & Adelong Times*: "During the visit it was pointed out by Warby that the record attempt would mean publicity for Tumut of multi-million dollar value". Lost in all the hype was a tiny story in the Perth *Daily News* in October that the State Department of Fisheries and Fauna had told Warby he couldn't run on Lake Dumbleyung because it would frighten away the wild life.

Then that month Warby had to postpone the December record attempt because the aerodynamic kit was still being built. By November, he was talking about January, 1976. The truth was that he still needed to find $12,000 to pay for the tailplane and the other fabrication work being done in the Bankstown (Sydney) factory of Hawker de Havilland. He even approached the Federal Government for help from the RAAF, but it was all getting lost within the bureaucracy. In January the Blowering course had been surveyed, with divers spending days clearing the water, but by now Warby was talking about March as the first run and a full attempt late in the year. In mid-February he named the date: March 13 and 14, 1976

A hard-hatted Warby as manager of the BHP lubrication department in Newcastle, 1970. He was still a "battler" trying to finance his boat racing.

Tradition demands the winner gets a dumping. Here Warby heads for the drink at the hands of crewmen Peter Cox (left) and Rex Crandall after a 1974 race.

One of the two RAAF surplus ex-Neptune bomber Westinghouse J34 jet engines Warby bought from the Federal Government for $100 each in 1969.

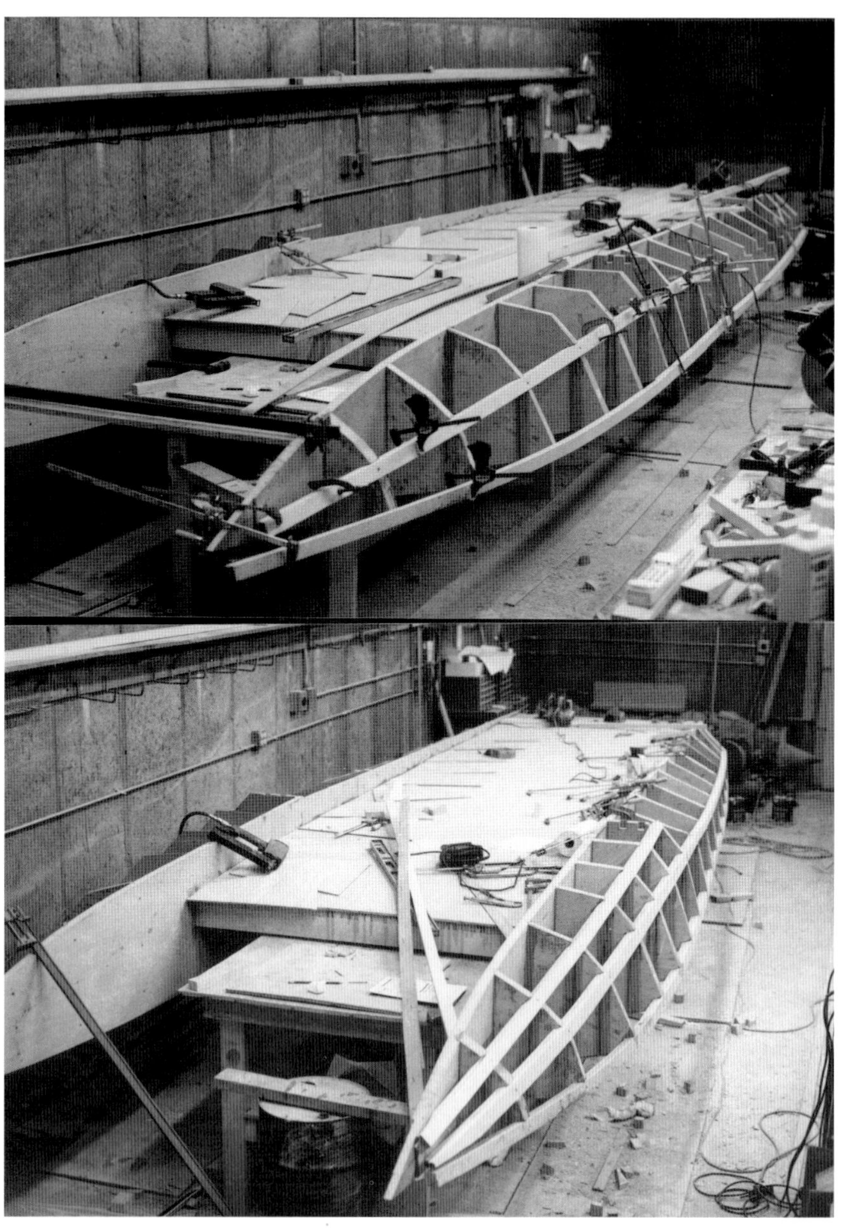

The partly-built hull of Spirit of Australia, showing the relatively straightforward design and the extensive use of timber, sitting in his garage.

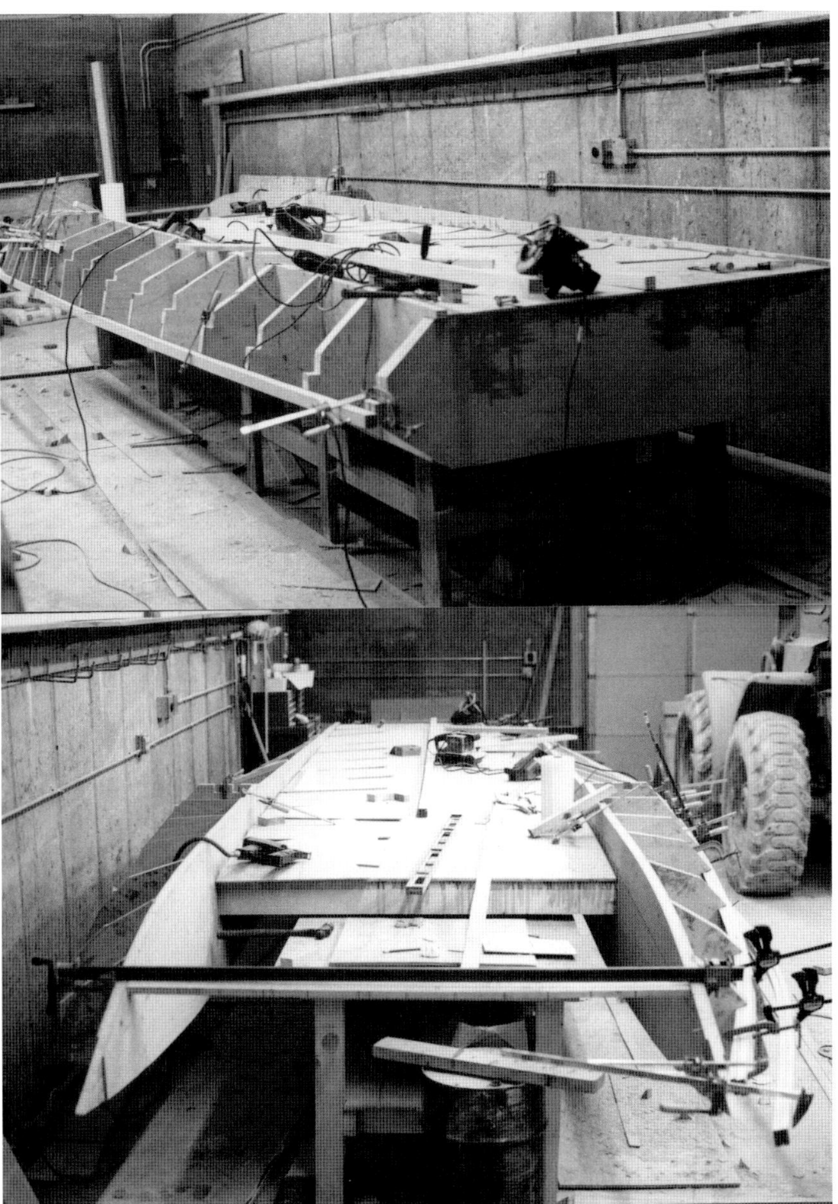

A conventional drag hydroplane, the hull was plywood over a spruce-and-oregon frame. Warby would later describe the design as "eyeball engineering".

The half-finished Spirit being readied for a test run at Taree's Manning River Aquatic Carnival in January, 1975. This was his favourite test river.

Shell Australia's legendary motor sport manager Archie White with the little-known boat racer at Warby's 1975 Sydney Motor Show painting stand.

Two of the significant men behind the record: Professor Tom Fink (left) with Warby and project manager Bob Apathy, after the event. Both have since died.

Lake Munmorah, near Newcastle, 1975, and a wonderful shot of the heat shimmer from the jet engine of the half-finished Spirit of Australia.

Spirit at Lake Munmorah for the low-speed pass. Note the position of the tailplane, later remade in aluminium and moved to the very rear of the boat.

Lake Blowering, near Tumut, finally selected for the record attempts. The Chamber of Commerce applauded, but the local boat club people obstructed.

The first run at Blowering in March, 1976; Tumut Chamber of Commerce president Graeme Thompson and Warby toast the day waist-deep in water.

Meeting and greeting at Tumut airport for the first Blowering inspection. Film-maker Rob McCauley is far left, Cyril Arnold of Shell next to him.

The old green International truck with the great boat on the trailer. The new tail-plane, fabricated by De Havilland, was ready for the first Blowering run.

November, 1976, and the Spirit is winched into the water. Warby's mother Evelyn, nervous and trembling as always, stands at the front of the boat.

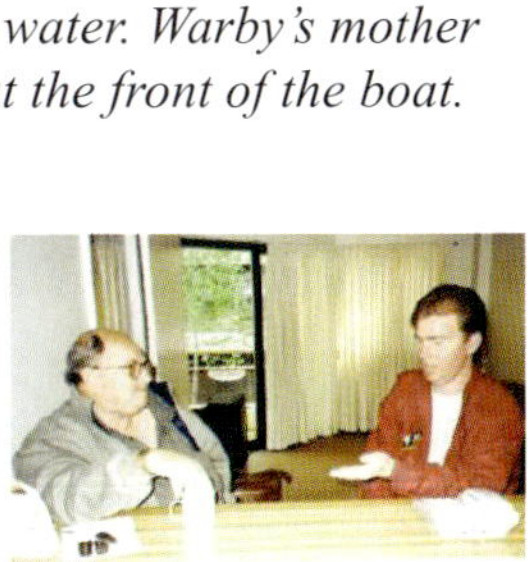

During the first Blowering run, Warby met for the first time the remarkable Major Robert Apathy, here with Ken's son David. Apathy would take control.

Sitting high in the cockpit to begin with, Warby guides the Fosseys boat away from the Blowering site, heading away towards the far turning point.

Brian Riley tethers the boat as Warby on the tailplane flashes the double-V sign after cracking the 10-year-old world record, November 20, 1977.

At full noise on Blowering: The Spirit "walked" a lot. "There's more to driving a boat than sitting in the cockpit like a bag of wet cement".

Not the picture of your average finely-tuned athlete, Warby pops the bubbly after the first successful record run. His mother was there, but not wife Jan.

The family together after the first record run. From left, Graeme Thompson, Ken's sister Ida, KW, his mother Evelyn and father, the quiet Neville.

American Lee Taylor, who at first refused to believe Warby's record or hand over the trophy, with the model of his "US Discovery II" that killed him.

The late and great Slim Dusty with one of his biggest fans. The International truck carried 23 Dusty cassettes Warby played endlessly on long trips.

Signing the Speedo contract in 1978 with chairman Bill McRae. Blue water yachtie McRae handed KW $60,000 for the first year of a three-year contract.

— but the boat still had the naked engine at the back and no superstructure.

By now the knockers were out in force. John Green, then president and former Commodore of the St George Motor Boat Club, the oldest and biggest such club in Australia, who had nominated Warby for membership, said in 1984 that some members wouldn't take Warby seriously. "They didn't understand his single-mindedness and motivation. His first world record run was received with the thunderous applause of a pin dropping. Later the knockers were walking around in their thongs and stubbies saying they knew he'd do it all along.". And then there was the Blowering boat club people, who bitterly resented being closed-out of the lake to allow this world speed record stupidity to interfere with their water skiing. Warby had negotiated with them on times and areas of the lake, because even a 5mph (8km/h) run across in a boat will produce a wash that will stay for maybe an hour, but several members told the press: "Tell Warby to go somewhere else — he's not wanted here".

Warby, cocky and big-mouthed as always, didn't help. On March 11 he was telling the press that the next day he would easily top 200 and more likely 230mph (370km/h). To make an event out of it, Shell had forked out more money to sponsor lesser class record attempts, and thus the full infrastructure was in place — the full-on communications and official timing team, police and emergency services, scuba divers, the military and civil defence, but the Spirit was still half-naked. Warby averaged only 177mph (282km/h) over two runs, and had to lift off when the boat started wanting to fly at just under 200mph (320km/h). He'd broken his own Australian record, and immediately predicted he'd break the world record in two months' time.

Once again, his mouth betrayed him, although he was as always, good for the quotable quotes. The Sydney *Sun* on March 17 had him saying: "All I want through any course is a quick time - not a meeting with the father of it"; and "Longevity runs in my family and I hope to keep it that way"; and "I do not want to meet death but I must admit, I am prepared to nod to it from a distance.....death catches up with all of us eventually, but I hope I'll be going too fast for it to reach me"; and the doozie of them all: "It is my philosophy that it is far better to have tried and died than not to have tried at all". This was Boy's Own stuff, straight from the Glorious Hero media manual.

The best thing that happened at Tumut that weekend was that he met Bob Apathy. "We were in the big marquee Shell had erected, discussing the next two days' planning and how the water would be best at daybreak, when out of the audience stepped Major Robert Apathy with his clipboard in hand. He proceeded to tell everyone not just what they were going to do but how they were going to do it, when they were going to do it and with whom. And we thought, this guy's really got his shit together. It was going to be run like a military manoeuvre and the Australian Power Boat Racing Association (APBA) record runs were never like that".

Apathy, 17 years in the Army, was the divisional officer of the St John's Ambulance Brigade in Canberra, a voluntary organisation that was doing everything down to supplying up to 30 divers for the operation. Said Warby later: "Bob was probably one of the coolest characters under pressure I've ever met in my life. I've always said he would crawl out of the rubble of a building demolished in an earthquake with a clipboard in his hand saying, step one, this is what we'll do. It wasn't long after that we decided he should take charge of the whole operation".

Apathy said later: "One of the reasons I went to Tumut was to find out whether he was on the level or not. It's very difficult when you haven't met a person to get involved in a project like this. I think one of the first things I asked him was whether he was a raving lunatic or whether he was fair dinkum. I think that established a real working relationship". He also found that despite the huge enthusiasm in Tumut for the record attempt, nobody knew how to co-ordinate things. "Both Ken and I felt pretty strongly about going at the record slowly and rationally rather than rushing it".

But still, there was the problem: There was no money in the till......

Spirit Was Not So Willing

Ken Warby, typically, got his next sponsorship money in the most bizarre ways. Film-maker and voluntary PR man Rob McCauley rang a man called Ken Berkeley, whom he hadn't seen for 20 years but was a leading light in sailing. Berkeley invited him to lunch in his boardroom. McCauley: "I hadn't seen him for 20 years, when we both had the arse out of our trousers, but here was his personal chef cooking us lunch in his board room. He had become a millionaire". McCauley told him about his involvement with this Ken Warby who has having a go at the world water speed record, and Berkeley looked at him hard and said: "Gee, that interests me - tell me more about it". McCauley said they had a few more drinks and later Berkeley came over to him and asked if Warby needed any financial help (Berkeley had apparently helped fund the young John Bertrand - later to win back the America's Cup - in his early yacht racing career).

Said McCauley later: "I said, 'Christ, does Warby need any help!' Berkeley said: 'I suppose he's talking hundreds of thousands' and I said, 'as a matter of fact he's looking for $7000 to buy a tailplane'. As I left he said: 'Tell this Ken Warby feller to come in Monday and I'll give him his $7000'. I looked at him in blank amazement and said, now look Ken, for God's sake, we haven't seen each other for 20 years and I've told you this story about this guy I'm involved with but it's no reason for you to give him $7000. And Ken said: 'Well, look, I've made a lot of money....there's lots of people have done things I wish I'd done....now I've got some money the least I can do is support those having a go'. Warby got his cheque Monday".

Then came another of those strokes of luck that typified Warby's life. Bernard Sheridan, then in his mid-fifties, the quiet, shy, tall and bespectacled general manager of an old-fashioned country clothing store chain called Fossey's, the last refuge of the pneumatic money tubes, saw on ABC television a program on Warby and the Spirit, which emphasised Warby's lack of sponsorship. He thought the company should be involved, and rang his boss George Coleman, managing director of the parent group, J.B. Young's, in Canberra. Neither was a boating man - Sheridan was rugby union and cricket and the closest Coleman came to the water was a holiday home on the coast at Bateman's Bay. Fossey's had only a small advertising budget and had never sponsored anything, but the unlikely pair met with Warby and Bob Apathy in their offices in Canberra.

Fossey's operations manager Warren Glenn, who was also there, said later: "It was certainly anything but a formal presentation. We thought we would see slides, charts and diagrams, but Ken in his quiet way just put it across to us". He showed them a model of the boat, and Coleman asked if $25,000 would help. That was about the company's total national advertising budget at the time. "It's incredible the exposure we got for that money", Glenn said. "The NSW Maritime Services Board produced hundreds of thousands of posters on safe boating with Fossey's on the boat, and we got one hour on ABC national television. Ken did personal tours for us later. We paid him $125 per store plus $25 for accommodation".

Warby was finally able to settle with the APBA, the Tumut Chamber of Commerce and local boating people, and his own demons on a weekend for his first record attempt - March 13-14, 1976. In hindsight, it was a stupid decision. The boat still didn't have its tailplane or engine cowlings, he was still trying to get Federal Government sanction for the back-door help he was getting from the Royal Australian Air Force (RAAF) technical training school, and there was so much media hype that everyone expected him to break the record every time the boat slid into the water. Every attempt cost the APBA money in surveyors, rescue crews, timing gear, referees, even a bond deposited with the international body - and the local ski club still hated him for stealing "their" lake.

Astonishingly, in a single run in a slight chop on the Saturday Warby cranked-off 319 km/h. However, as with a land speed record a return run within one hour is needed to establish the average bid time, and Warby was determined to hasten slowly; in any case, the time on the lake was limited as the APBA had taken advantage of the access to

Blowering to bring in three other boats and drivers to attack other category records. On the Sunday Warby was timed at 315.4 km/h on the first run but at just on 320 in the second the boat started to get airborne. He backed-off, and when he went through the traps at the other end the net average was 283.2 km/h, a new Australian record but well away from the world's. The headlines trumpeted: "Jet ace Ken streaks home", and "World record in his sights", but that was far from the truth.

Warby now started talking about September, but he was threatening to take the attempt away from Blowering. The Tumut Chamber of Commerce had promised $12,000 in sponsorship to boost the program, but didn't say it was going to try and raise it by an art union or lottery, and there was some growing local cynicism about the whole thing. The Fossey's sponsorship came just in time. By October Warby was able to reach agreement with the Tumut people and target November 20-21 as the weekend for the first serious attempt with the new tailfin and cowling, which became a suitable canvas for the Fossey's name, along with a new Latin motto: "Animo et Fide". By this time, too, the people around Warby had coined the phrase "Project 300" for the attempt, 300 mph (483km/h) the target above Taylor's world record of 285.213mph (351.1km/h).

To his credit, Warby tried to damp-down the hype. On the Friday (November 19), he said that because it was the boat's first run with the T-shaped tailplane he would work it up from slower speeds but would be happy to top 200 mph (322 km/h) for another new Australian record. But the

Monday headlines rang the warning bells: "Spirit was not so willing", and "Record bid fails".

It had started badly for Warby anyway when a stone broke the windscreen of his old green truck towing the Spirit. The next day, Warby in the cockpit for the first time in nearly seven months and with the wind rippling the water, the Spirit sat there and sulked. When the batteries died, Apathy brought in two generators and jumper leads and eventually it fired. But the water was rough, and he went through the surveyed one-kilometre course on one-third throttle at 172 (280), slowing to around 130 past the spit of land where the press cameras perched. But on the Sunday nothing would persuade the Westinghouse to fire; it turned out to be a 20-cent rubber O-ring in the fuel igniter. The APBA timekeepers and referees had an equally frustrating weekend, engine problems sending the light aircraft flying them to Tumut into a forced landing in an asparagus paddock.

Warby told the media he wouldn't return to the lake until probably March the next year, 1977. "Whilst I need several more trials - it could take half a dozen weekends on the lake before Spirit is ready for the world attempt - I am pleased with the way the tailplane felt and feel it is definitely making it a much more stable boat. What I need is a chance to make the exact adjustments. It's like the suspension on a racing car - it will take time out on the circuit to sort it out and get it spot-on". What he didn't say was that the tailplane had developed five degrees of twist during the run and now had to be remade. And the boat still didn't have the necessary air scoops both sides of the cockpit.

But he still had to do the publicity appearances, brief blasts across the national capital Canberra's Lake Burley Griffin (normally banned to all powered craft) and up the Manning River in the annual Australia Day Taree Aquatic Festival. He started towing the Spirit to personal appearances at Fossey's country stores, in towns with names like Lithgow and Parkes and Forbes and Dubbo and Cootamundra, Goulburn, Griffith and Queanbeyan. But the pressure was on him, and he was forced to nominate April 16-17 as the weekend for the first serious record attempt.

The Water Skiers are Revolting

Warby was inflexible in his workup timetable. Later he would list the mileposts as achieving (in miles per hour) 166, 178, 196, 225 and 245. "There's more to driving a boat than sitting in the cockpit like a bag of wet cement", he would say. Spirit would "walk around" a lot - the term is "sponson walk" - and he would let it have its head. "At 80 it would kick out its tail but you had to get through that. At 200 the boat used to have a little twitch as it went through".

The whole process started with the Spirit in the water, alongside a 12-foot aluminium "tin dish" loaded with batteries, a standard NATO aircraft power-up plug connector, and safety equipment. Warby initiated the starting procedure by pressing a button on the dash that spun the engine to 10% speed before he hit the igniter button - "just like lighting a gas stove", Warby said. "Then you switch on the fuel and crack the throttle open and within a few seconds you have a fire in the engine. You then get 35% power, which is idle in a J34, and the boat is starting to move slowly in the water....just a few knots. At 30% you give the wave-off signal and they pull out the power plug and go like hell to get away out of there. If their motor stalled the standard instruction was to dive overboard as deep as they could.

"The boat would be down in the water, just bellying along. I'd slide up in the seat a foot or so, so I could look around through 360 degrees to see everything and I'd stay there to the start point so I could see over the nose of the boat. I'd ease the boat up onto the plane around 90-100, but I had a marker down near the dam wall where I'd turn at 60 mph and line up on a marker way down at Yellowfin Bay. I could see the power lines across, marking the narrow neck of the lake, and then when I was confident I had the boat lined-up I'd settle back down and mash the throttle — but not full, because with the J34 that could over-fuel the engine. You could hear it growl behind you as if annoyed, but you'd give it a good footfull and if everything felt all right you'd go.

"There was three miles to run to the first marker. The faster you went the faster the acceleration was, like 100-200 was a lot slower than 200-300. The main thing was to keep the boat trimmed. The second marker was two spits of land - I didn't want buoys or anything out on the course". Down in Yellowfin Bay, 10 miles from the dam wall, would wait another boat crew, this time with a complete refuelling load of kerosene, and to handle the turnaround for the necessary second run.

Several things could kill Warby in those 10 miles. The crew had constantly swept and combed the water for even the tiniest bits of debris, and no boats were allowed on Blowering from dawn, because even a small runabout will create a wake that will for an hour or more leave corrugations in the water. This was exactly what would happen before the first serious run. Warby: "There had always been antagonism from the Blowering Boat Club, who weren't very receptive to me using what they considered their water. It was only a few people - one in particular - and some of it was jealousy, some thought I was an idiot, some I was disturbing their quiet haven.

"I had arranged for the water skiers to use an area down towards the dam where they wouldn't disturb the actual run area but some still weren't happy. The locals and the ski boaties thought that every time we went down there we'd get a record and that would be the end of it". One said to the press: "Tell Warby to go somewhere else - he's not welcome here", and when asked why the locals wouldn't support the world record attempt he said straight to camera: "Stiff shit". The weird thing about Spirit, however, was that Warby had designed it not for smooth water - as all previous record-runners had done - but for a chop of between three and six inches. "We could handle that if it was evenly spaced. If you can imagine a sheet of corrugated iron you can run across that because the boat will stretch across it evenly, but if in the middle someone puts a higher lump it becomes a launching ramp".

On April 17 Warby finally put it to them for the first time. But even then the locals gave problems. On the

Saturday night, before the record attempt the next morning, someone cut through the master timing cable. The timing points were located a kilometre apart with the cable going under the water, but accessible from something as light as a rowboat. Warby had even agreed to be off the water by midday Sunday so the locals could still get their water-skiing time. On the Saturday his two-way average was 193.17 mph (310.8 km/h). On Sunday he finished his first run at 11.32 am, and the second at 11.45, but wasn't happy and asked the local Maritime Services Board officer for dispensation to do a third run — "Hey, I really didn't think anyone would mind". But the local boating club immediately lodged a complaint with the officer and threatened to report him to his superiors, so that was that.

Meanwhile, people were starting to get worried about him. Leo Villa, who worked with Sir Malcolm Campbell on his cars and boats and later as chief engineer for son Donald, had been communicating with Warby with audio tapes, and had told him he wished he had built a metal boat instead of a wooden one. On one message he says: "I do sincerely think....I'm sure...that the actual stresses particularly the impact loadings at the speeds we're talking about, you can't treat the matter of strength too lightly". Neither did he think the big tailfin was necessary, because he believed it would create lift instead of downforce and preferred a shaped keel to keep the nose down. But he deferred to Fink's knowledge: "He knows what he's talking about. He's a very clever boy". But then he added: "He hasn't cracked 250 yet. That's when his trouble starts".....

Interviewed in 1984, Fink calmly explained the physics. "You get to a speed where the downward force of the boat is equalled by the lift generated by the speed. The boat at rest is under atmospheric pressure.....but as soon as you switch-on the engine and you have a fire in the combustion chamber the pressure is greater than the atmosphere and the boat wants to get out but it can't. So at the rear that pressure is pushed out because there is nothing to stop it. The movement of the boat is merely a manifestation of the force within".

He goes on: "Cycling at top speed you think there's a wind even on a dull, quiet day. So you bend down to present less of yourself to the wind. You want to cycle faster but you can't, so you put on an engine.......if you want to go 10 times faster you must have 100 times the thrust, or push or power. All you need is a bigger and bigger engine to increase the horizontal component. But there is a vertical component. There will be a speed when the vertical force is equal to the weight and it is ready to take off....a tiny bit faster and there will be a net lift upwards. And there is one unfortunate thing about boats and planes - the force mightn't act where you want it to act".

This, said Fink, was the problem with Campbell's Bluebird. "I estimated he would be killed at 315-325 mph, although he could travel quite safely at 280 mph. It all looked quite suicidal, really". He said Bluebird had been designed to run only on glass-smooth water and was very susceptible to pitching oscillations, when the bow and stern go up at different moments, or periods (which is what killed Cobb at 200 mph). Into that the designers must also factor things like yaw moments.

Fink said both Campbell's boat and Warby's had about the same "wetted length" (that is, the amount of hull actually touching the water at the rear). "But Warby had somehow evolved a hull form which was very cunning in that it almost trapped an air cushion in the space under the hull that served to damp-out these oscillations". He also said Warby had recognised the need to get the boat up on the plane as soon as possible because all lakes had a finite length, and his boat had very good damping of pitch oscillations. "But all that is still not enough. You must look at secondary things like rolling oscillations, or tramping around a longitudinal axis. It's like a plumb bob hanging from a string - it does nothing until you pull it and let go. The Romans knew everything in a mechanical system that had an amplitude of oscillation. The Romans discovered resonance in soldiers marching across a bridge, so soldiers since then have been ordered to break step crossing a bridge". (The same analogy was raised in 1997 during the controversy over the collapse of a temporary bridge leading to the Maccabean Games in Tel Aviv in Israel, when five Australian athletes died in the disaster).

So why did Warby's boat go better on a choppy surface? Here we're talking fluid dynamics - and remember that in 1977 it was less a science than a black art that few understood, a region where few had gone. Fink later explained that a regular swell sets up undulations and resonance, where a chop was irregular, "a sort of fast intermittent hammering", too high a frequency to start the boat oscillating. He said Warby's boat could run up to 200 mph in waves a foot high, but the only danger was the "bit of plywood", the wedge, and the stresses on that. But Warby's enormous experience in building wooden boats negated that risk.

Interestingly, Fisk rejected the notion that Campbell held, that aeronautic design should play a part in the boat. "The pragmatic experience developed by high-speed aircraft pilots didn't really help one jot. This enterprise is much closer to the other end, where pragmatism really plays quite a big part when handled by an intelligent pragmatic like Warby, who observed over his 20 years of power boats all the characteristics of behaviour of water and air to come up with something that was pretty good and didn't need much help". He said Campbell relied on outside experts to design and build his boat. "He had certain strong wishes that were irrational. He wanted the layout of the cockpit, engine, and air intakes to look like the-then generation of fighter aircraft". It was the rearward layout of the air intakes, as we have seen, that killed him.

But by the middle of 1997, Ken Warby was thinking about an afterburner.....

And Now, A Dead Duck

Leo Villa had calculated that with the Spirit weighing around 3.2 tonnes it would need 5000 pounds of thrust to get it over 300 mph (482km/h) "which struck me as being a bit on the shallow side. I did learn from a tape Ken sent me that he was hoping to fit an afterburner, in which case he would have another 50% more power up his sleeve. Mind you old Ken will have some trouble with it. He hasn't cracked 250 yet - that's when his trouble starts", repeated Villa.

By September, 1977 the boat was virtually finished, with the air scoops in place, and Warby had installed an afterburner. On the Wednesday (October 27) before he was to make his first serious attempt he towed the outfit to Fairbairn RAAF base in Canberra and said to a public relations officer: "Look, I've got a jet engine in a boat out here; do you mind if we take it down the back of the paddock and give it a run?" The nonplussed officer introduced him to two Flight Sergeants, Peter Lyzun and Peter Dorman, who took him to the jet engine runup pad.

"But we couldn't get the afterburner to light", the eternally-laconic Warby said later. "We were shearing drives to various pumps. Then we hit real trouble. I'd left a screwdriver on the boat and it vibrated down into the engine. I got onto Bob Apathy on CB radio and said: 'We've got a minor technical problem'. He said: 'What's wrong, Uncle?' I said: 'We've just destroyed the engine'. In good CB talk he said: 'Would you give me a 10-nine on that?' I said: 'We've just destroyed the engine'. He said: 'Oh, it sounds like we've got a minor technical problem'." The screwdriver came out as tiny steel balls, but the engine never missed a beat, even though Warby was nearly at full throttle. He didn't know what damage had been done until he looked down the intake and saw the minced-up turbine blades.

By seven o'clock in the evening Warby decided they had to get hold of the $65 engine that was lying on the dirt under the trees in his backyard at Concord - an engine he had once almost given away. Film-maker McCauley and Apathy jumped into Warby's old green International truck and took off on the four-hour drive north. They got there about 1am. "There were grape and pumpkin vines growing all over it", said McCauley. "We rigged up a light and heaved the engine with chains onto the back of the truck. We got back about 6am and they had taken out the other engine and the RAAF blokes were standing by to drop in this rusty old thing".

The RAAF techs and Warby worked all day to install it, and miraculously it fired first time. But they still couldn't get the afterburner to light. McCauley was shooting a documentary for the ABC. The crew set up 100 metres aft, looking up the tailpipe. McCauley got sick of the delays and decided to shoot the ignition from the side. Warby: "The very next time I lit the afterburner it was on for about eight seconds and threw flames so far it lit a grass fire 10 metres behind where McCauley had been standing. If he'd still been there he would have done well to learn the words to 'Mammy'. What had happened was that a fuel line had split and caught fire. It was the only shot the afterburner ever fired".

Warby decided to run the rusty old engine without the afterburner and he, Fink and McCauley took off at 11 on the Friday night towing the boat. It was freezing cold, the only blessing that the truck's cassette player had gone out to lunch and Warby couldn't play Slim Dusty. Fink became fascinated by the CB radio. Said Warby: "I was driving along talking to all the truckies going past. Tom got fascinated by that, so here we had this prof with 47 letters after his name learning CB lingo".

Nobody was awake when they rolled into the frost-covered camp at Hume's Crossing - named after one of the pair of explorers who opened up the country between Sydney and Melbourne - on the edge of the Blowering lake around 2am. Warby got in the back of the truck, pulled some canvas over him and got about two hours' sleep - his first since Wednesday morning. At 5am he found cook John McInerney with the fire going and breakfast on the go. "He was great. On the record attempts he would do 4-500 meals a weekend.....rescue teams, boat pushers, mechanics, the press, the public....anyone who turned up got a feed".

Warby went out on the lake a couple of hours later. On the run-in he radioed Apathy that there was a flock of birds - duck or black shag - on the path ahead, but Apathy told him not to worry, they'd just taken off. "But then I felt a jar and I knew I'd hit one". That damaged the rudder mounting, so they put the boat back on the trailer and headed into Tumut to a Shell dealer with a good workshop to repair it. Back in the gathering dusk on the lake he ran the boat up to 220 mph (354 km/h), but he knew he had a sick engine behind him. On the Sunday he clocked a new Australian record of 245.82 mph (394.6 km/h), with a cracked fuel tank and able only to fill to half the boat's 320-litre capacity. But they were still 40 mph (60 km/h) to take the world mark away from Lee Taylor. Warby called a full-on record attempt for three weeks away.

Warby, was, however, starting to have a conversation with this boat. In his orange pressure suit with the inflated Mae West, the big engineer was jammed into a narrow cockpit reclining at 150 degrees, the tiny drilled-alloy-spoked steering wheel down between his knees, big black goggles on, the microphone from his helmet radio curving around his mouth and under his chin a green button release for the ejector seat. He had a half canopy, or windscreen, rejecting a full canopy with the strange words that it scared him, that he'd rather leave the boat in a full flip-over.

The Blowering run at full water was just over 14 kilometres long. The start sequence was to flick on the fuel and igniter switches, then fire the engine, and 10-12 seconds later the long stab of red flame would erupt from the tail. The engine settled down to idle at 4500 of its 12,500 rpm, and Warby would gently nudge it out onto the open water - too much right foot too early and he would dump excess fuel into the engine and perhaps burn-out a turbine. At this stage he was reading the exhaust gauge temperature more than anything else, and gradually increasing the revs. The speed was being read by the aircraft-style pitot tube in the nose.

Once Spirit was at the dam wall Warby would do a wide U-turn and line up the entrance to Yellowfin Bay. He had six kilometres to run before hitting the first timing marker for the measured kilometre, being recorded electronically by an underwater line between two sets of surveyed concrete markers on both sides running the timing equipment, backed by two separate sets of stopwatches doing different checking tasks. Warby would concentrate on holding the boat on line while allowing it to "walk" a bit, calling the speeds on his CB radio as the markers flashed past and checking three other gauges - exhaust temperature, oil pressure and tachometer. He told one interviewer: "I know that if the rudder turns more than one quarter of a degree, the stern of the Spirit will try to meet the bow and I'll meet my Maker".

What was it all for anyway? To get your name on a silver plaque on the black wooden base supporting a solid silver statue of Boadicea, the legendary English fighting queen. It is said to be valued at around $50,000. The inscription reads: "This trophy was presented in 1870 by HRH the

Prince of Wales, afterwards King Edward VII, for open competition by schooners. In 1934 it was discovered in an old silversmith's shop in Kent (UK) and after renovation by the original makers was presented by Mr T.B. Andre to the Royal Motor Yacht Club. In 1937 the club allocated the trophy to be retained by the holder for the time being of the World Water Speed Record". The plaques read, in chronological order:

- Sir Malcolm Campbell, Lake Maggiore, September, 1937, 129.5 mph.
- 1938 Sir Malcolm Campbell, Bluebird, 130.9 mph.
- 1939 Sir Malcolm Campbell, Bluebird, 141.74 mph.
- 1950 Stanley Sayers, Slo-Moshun, 160.323 mph.
- 1952 Stanley Sayers, Slo-Moshun IV, 178.497 mph.
- July 13, 1955, Donald Campbell, Bluebird, 202.32 mph.
- November 16, 1955, Donald Campbell, Bluebird, 216.5 mph.
- September 19, 1956, Donald Campbell, Bluebird, 225.63 mph.
- November 10, 1958, Donald Campbell, Bluebird, 248.62 mph.
- May 14, 1959, Donald Campbell, Bluebird, 260.35 mph.
- December 31, 1964, Donald Campbell, Bluebird, 276.34 mph.
- June 30, 1967, Lee Taylor Jr, Hustler, 285.213 mph.

Says Warby: "A lot of people have died for it. But it's an inanimate object made out of silver. It's like a cemetery. All the men who have held the record have died trying to raise it. I can hold an annual reunion of the world's most exclusive club wherever I am in the world, because I'm the only member".

At the end of the return run on the Sunday Spirit had gone through the traps still accelerating past 285 mph. For the record attempt three weeks away someone had taped a note to the boat's dash. It read: "Hit 300, then smile"…….

That Extra Half-Inch

They were back at Hume's Crossing on Friday, November 18. Professor Tom Fink was there again, turtleneck sweater under white overalls, neatly combed silver hair and rimless glasses. In the pocket of the overalls was a small calculator. "What came out of that thing was incredible", Warby would say. But it couldn't get the afterburner to work - Fink was always a bit nervous about that thing, particularly the difficulty of shutting it off in a hurry - and on the Saturday the best Warby could manage was 251mph ((403.8km/h} on the first run from the launching place at The Pines, and 257 (413.5) on the return. There was only a handful of press people there – including author Bill Tuckey - along with a few supporters from the St George Motor Boat Club, but a lot of the local boaties, particularly the skiers who were still bitching loudly about being kept off "their" water. They were heartily sick of what they saw as Warby's failures.

Warby: "At lunchtime we got into my caravan and Tom started arguing that if we didn't have enough power without the afterburner we had to reduce the drag. On that bloody calculator he worked out that the rudder alone was causing 2400 pounds of drag at 300mph (480km/h). If we cut off two inches (5cm) this would reduce by 400 pounds, which would give us another 400 pounds of thrust". It would, the calculator told them, lift the potential speed to 280. But Fink warned this would be dangerous, reducing the safety margin because the rudder helped hold down the boat's nose. Warby, as always, made the quick, pragmatic decision.

The boat was trailered back to the Shell service station where they had fixed the previous damage, and with an oxy-acetylene torch - a "hot axe" – Warby got to work. "Tom had said two inches but I cut off an extra half an inch (1.2cm) just for luck. I couldn't find any safety goggles so I did the cutting with one eye closed to reduce the risk of spatter. I finished it off on a rotary grinder and we got back to camp about midnight". They had also reduced the exhaust outlet to raise exhaust temperature by 45 degrees, promising an extra 170 pounds of thrust. Between Warby and Fink they had worked out that because Ken was already over-revving the engine by four percent, which upped the temperature by 50 degrees, they could reduce the outlet diameter by three-eighths of an inch (1.2cm) and lift the temperature another 45 degrees - it actually worked out at 50 degrees.

He would laugh later that the extra half-inch got him the world record by three miles-per-hour. On the first run on that momentous Sunday morning – the last day of the year his agreement made the lake available to him - he clocked 290-plus on the out leg, and Warby saw 300 on the return leg. As they towed him in, Warby convinced he had done it, they gave him the average - 276mph (440km/h), or 10mph (16km/h) under Taylor's mark. "I sort of went back to the boat a little upset, telling the timing officials I thought they were wrong". He yelled at the crew to fuel-up Spirit again. There's a classic piece of film footage of him storming back to the boat shouting "Well, we've got Campbell, now let's go and get that other bastard!" Lee Taylor heard about that later and was less than impressed, although "bastard" in Australia can often be used in affection.

"Just before I got in the boat they told me I had actually averaged 286 (460kmh), but to get the record you had to beat it by three-quarters of one percent, so I was still 0.9 mph short. So I got back in and took off; it was about 9.30 or 10am, and it started to rain. As I slowed down at the end of the first run I had done a bad one, because the rain was coming onto the windscreen like bullets". He had run only 266 (428km/h). He told the crew to cancel that out, and they refuelled him from the fuel boat as he waited almost an hour for the rain to ease off. Then he booted it, and he hit 300 and smiled. "I did 302. I was absolutely wrapped - the first time anyone was officially timed over 300".

All he needed on the return run, which had to be done within an hour, was 287 mph (461.7km/h). But while he was being refuelled one of the local ski boats, called "Screwer 2" - a name that has gone down in infamy in motor boating circles - did a speed run across the lake. Enraged Warby supporters confronted the owner, screaming abuse at him, but he responded with the "it's our fucking lake" tirade. Film-maker Rob McCauley: "I grabbed the crew and the microphone and spoke to the young guy who made remarks like 'Warby's a shit' and 'why should he have the lake?' and 'who the hell does he think he is?'. It had all the makings of a disaster. The record was so close and this fuckwit and his mate had almost spoiled it". What many people don't realise is that once created, a wash stays for a long time. Hitting even a small one at 300 mph can launch into the air a hydroplane sitting on a contact patch about the size of the palms of two hands. "But I had to go back, knowing there was a lump out there but not knowing how big it was", said Warby. "But one thing was for sure; I was going to have a big go. I went into the kilometre at 255 and jarred the boat as it hit the wash so I backed off a bit".

McCauley was back out on the course in two boats with his film crew. "The first run was from the dam wall end of the lake and the boat was bloody flying. It was totally unreal....a grey, grey day and this big boat sponson-walking all the way down that course....faster than it had ever gone before. When Warby turned back in anger to get back into the boat my heart was in my mouth because he was out to prove something. That was a wrong motivation for me, and I was quite frightened as he went out. It was probably the most frightening time in the whole project, but it does show what Warby is all about. That was a magic afternoon."

Warby's seat in the boat had an ejector mechanicsm, but as he had said before the run: "At 600 feet a second you're dead, minced and buried before you can press any button". He sat with his ungloved hands at 10 to two on the wheel, his right foot planted on a huge accelerator pedal shaped to fit his boot. He wore goggles under the helmet visor because the wind at 200 mph was trying to rip away the visor. Asked what it had felt like at those speeds he said: "I really don't know. I remember absolutely total concentration on the instruments and the line of the boat and cursing because I was being buffetted by the wind. But it's more a mechanical challenge. You don't just drive that boat, you wear it. If it twitches you feel it right through your body".

The Australian Power Boating Association (APBA) officials and the official referee from the International Motor Boating Union, Theo Felstead, took almost two hours to check and re-check the equipment and their calculations, because it was so close to the record. Warby, still in his overalls, walked up to McCauley and put both hands on his shoulder and said: "Mate, we've done it. It's not official, but I hear we've done it". He wasn't jumping up and down. He was immersed in a quiet, almost shy aura of satisfaction.

His grey-haired mother, Sal, was the first one he went up to when he jumped off the Spirit. "She came down to the water's edge and I put my arm around her and headed for the radio shack. She was shaking, and I told her to stop and she said she couldn't. I said I was the one who should be shaking. She was a natural-born worrier. While we were waiting for the official word I said to her: 'Come sit on my knee; I've sat on yours enough'. But she just shook and shook and shook, with tears running down her face". Warby's father was also there, in his favorite hat and cardigan, smiling a lot but avoiding showing much emotion, but Ken's wife Jan and their three sons, Peter (then 13), David (9) and Michael (8), were not. "I refused point-blank to let them come to Blowering. I didn't want the family to go through it. But Jan didn't want to go anyway. I think now she saw the Spirit run only once. She had a real phobia about the media, about being interviewed. I guess one clown in the family's enough".

Eventually the officials called in Tom Fink and his intrepid calculator, and he confirmed their figure - it was a new record at 288.172 mph (463.668 km/h). When it was announced to about 100 people at the base camp a triumphant roar went up. It had happened. After all these years, after all the disappointments, all the penny-pinching, all the sleepless nights, all the flak from the Warby Knockers' Club and some of the local boat people, all the ignorance of the media, all the knockbacks from potential sponsors, it had happened. Warby had not only taken the record from Taylor; he was the first man to design, build and drive the boat to do it. This time the big city media did take notice, and the stories of the 10-year struggle, the boat designed on a kitchen table, the rusty jet engine lying in the backyard, were told and retold. McCauley's great documentary, called "Hit 300 And Smile" was aired on ABC television.

McCauley: "My feeling immediately afterwards was that he'd survived. He'd come out of that afternoon, that strange day, when all sorts of strange things were happening.....he was alive and the boat was in one piece and whether or not he had or had not got the record didn't seem to matter. He'd broken into a realm of magic that afternoon and he's risen above so much as a person. When the record was announced everyone went a bit berserk. There were lots of tears in lots of eyes. It was just like a big school picnic where the local team had had a win and everybody felt part of it......this small group of people on a patch of ground on the edge of a lake in the country, going out of their minds........"

But the glory was short-lived.

Enter Speedo and the RAAF

That Sunday night Warby and others drove to Bob Apathy's home in Canberra for more celebrations. "Even though we'd broken the world record we still had to pack-up the camp - nobody's going to do that for you", Warby said. "The world doesn't stop just because you break a record. You get all the shouting and adulation and suddenly it's all gone and you're on your own again". He and Apathy were the last to leave, towing Spirit behind the old green Inter. "It was a really weird feeling lying in bed that night, thinking, shit, what are you going to do tomorrow? Because I had never thought past breaking the record. It was simple bloody-mindedness, tunnel vision, whatever you want to call the bloody thing. I had no idea what I would do for a living. I had originally said that once I got the record I would fly to Birdsville in the outback and sit on the verandah of the Birdsville pub drinking champagne and waiting for the media phone calls".

They seldom came. The feat didn't make the front pages of the metropolitan dailies, partly because the Canberra press gallery, the closest bunch of hot shots, had abandoned Blowering Dam on that weekend to trail the-then Prime Minister, Malcolm Fraser, south to Tasmania for his launching of a new election campaign. "I took the boat back to Concord and stuffed it into the backyard. The St George Motor Boat Club put on a hell of a presentation night for me". It was the privilege of the three-times World Champion of Formula One, Sir Jack Brabham (who had moved into the area after his retirement), to hand him the official world record certificate.

But governments did nothing - although the Melbourne Tourism Authority conferred on him the title of Ambassador For The City, mainly because of his support for the Melbourne Boat Show, the biggest in Australia. He had problems with the APBA, mainly with paperwork, even though the association's own referees and the international observer had been at Blowering. "They printed a certificate listing the speed but not mentioning the record. They were a bunch of clowns, less interested in competitors than in fighting with the various State bodies, and I got caught in the middle of a dogfight. There was even an attempt by one or two of the APBA people to declare the record invalid". In fact, the world record was approved on December 27, 1977, by the international body (who sent him a bill for $70 for the certificate). Even the influential US *Powerboat* magazine gave the story just a few paragraphs on page six. Boating writer Graeme Andrews wrote to all the editors of the North American boating mags offering words and color photography. He got no takers.

However, Lee Taylor knew about it. On November 25 he wrote to Warby: "It is my pleasure to congratulate you for successfully setting a new world water speed record. Now with its fresh world-wide recognition, which it so rightfully deserves, it will naturally create public anticipation for its future. My past record time sheets have been enclosed. I would be very thankful if you would send to me copy(sic) of your timed runs and picture or pictures of your present record-holding craft". Former world land speed record holder Gary ("Rocket Man") Gabelich, the first man to break the 200 mph barrier in a quarter-mile supercharged nitro-burning hydro drag boat in 1969, also wrote, adding: "I must say that 200 mph-plus in an open cockpit boat felt much faster than going 650 mph on land!"

But Warby had become a bitter man. By mid-January he was telling the press his next goal was to be the first to take the record over a two-way average of 300 mph (483 km/h) but that this time he wouldn't do it for glory - he wanted money. "I couldn't believe Australians were so insensitive to a countryman breaking the world water speed record. My performance hardly made news. Well I'm not hanging around for the same thing to happen again. I'm going to push the speed record over the 300 mph average and the chances are it will be in another country where foreign sponsors will benefit". In an interview published in Australian *Pol* magazine in April, 1978, he said: "The boat is open now for the highest bidder. It doesn't matter whether it's Idi Amin wanting it as his flagship for the

Ugandan Navy. I've done my bit for God and country and got yawned at. Now I can go out and make a buck".

A man whose pragmatism doesn't always extend to doing the correct sums, he had finally worked out that his long road to the record had cost a bit more than $90,000 and of that, sponsors had contributed only $20,000. Australian *Powerboat* magazine in that January wrote: "It's a sad indictment of Australians and their attitude towards one of their own kind". ABC television gave its prestigious "Sportsman Of The Year" award to someone else, letting it be known that Warby had run a close second. The Newcastle *Sun* boating writer, John Norris, wrote: "Ken Warby - this country is not big enough for you, you will have to leave.....unfortunately it seems Ken Warby is not going to get the recognition he deserves and the backing he needs right here in his own country. To date he has declined offers from Italy, Britain and the US because he wants the world water speed record to be wholly Australian. Perhaps he should reconsider".

The final humiliation came when Warby asked Qantas to compensate him for using the slogan "Spirit Of Australia", which he had registered and owned as a trademark for the boat, or for Qantas to use the name with sponsorship in "contra". The airline refused, finally paying him a sum he now calls a pittance. Around the same time the now-disgraced former entrepreneur Alan Bond was spending millions of dollars of sponsors' money on repeated attempts to lift the America's Cup, the "ugly mug" that has relevance mainly to billionaires.

Warby was repeatedly asked whether he would try to elevate the record. He told a couple of journalists that on one run he had seen 345mph (555km/h) - which was simply not true - but that he was under pressure to run again. "Next time I run, every man and his dog is letting me know they're going to be there. I think from the last count we had 32 news reporters who are going to be there. It's the good old Australian system; it's easy to back a winner, especially after the first run". By March the Sydney *Sun* newspaper was saying Warby would run the Spirit with an afterburner at Blowering the next month, the target 750 km/h.

Then came some daylight. In June, 1978, Warby was awarded the MBE in the Queen's Birthday Honours list. The Melbourne Boat Show in July, 1978, featured the Spirit and Warby as its star attraction. One of the crowd was Bill McRae, chairman of the famous Speedo swimwear company, which had always been involved in water sports, particularly the Olympic and Commonwealth Games. McRae had competed in the world-famous Sydney-Hobart blue-water yacht classic and saw Spirit for the first time at the show. He and Warby hit it off immediately. He asked Warby to see him at his Artarmon (Sydney) office, and Warby walked out with $60,000 for the first year's sponsorship. Far fatter than the Fossey's (nevertheless vital) input, it would run for three years.

"I think the whole thing was well organised", McRae would say later. "We were very happy with the whole association". So keen was the McRae family after the second record was set that they started planning a tour with

Warby and the boat to Europe - possibly to run on Lake Coniston - and Moscow, to coincide with the 1980 Olympics. Then the Australian Government joined other nations in boycotting the Moscow games, and that was the end of that. But Sydney's Channel Ten TV station had thrown in money for exclusive rights to the second attack.

This galvanised Warby. By July, he was talking October at Blowering. He had been to the US for the first time, talking to possible sponsors as well as meeting Lee Taylor, and it was a smoother-groomed, better-manicured Warby who came back, now 39 years old, and knowing that Taylor was nearly finished building US Discovery II, a 40-foot (12.2 metres) long behemoth bearing a hydrogen-peroxide-powered rocket with 8500 pounds of thrust backed by 37 sponsor companies. Warby thrives on challenge, and this was all he needed. But as always happens with sporting sponsorship, there is no such thing as a free lunch.

In the interim the Royal Australian Air Force (RAAF) had upped its particular involvement in supporting Warby's second attack. By September, the RAAF had officially sanctioned the use of its apprentice training program at its base at Forest Hill, a suburb of a southern NSW town with the appealing name of Wagga Wagga, to work on rebuilding Warby's J34 engines. It had only just been introduced as the training engine for the Wagga technical training school, which had the only J34 test bed in Australia. Warby moved the boat and the three engines into the hangar at Forest Hill, to be worked on by apprentices who at 15-17 years old had signed on for nine years for seven trade courses. The J34 engines had been used mainly as JATOs (jet-assisted takeoffs) to boost the turbo-props on the anti-submarine Neptunes, now phased out, but the J34 was regarded as an ideal training tool.

The commanding officer of the base, Group Captain Bob Bartram, was a dynamic character who was among other things a member of the Wagga Wine And Food Society. Warby had been a guest speaker at one of their functions after he had set the new world record. Bartram invited him to inspect the base facility, and Warby was awestruck by the array of engines. The officer who ran the show, maintenance manager Flight Lieutenant Dave Appleby, had two instructors, Stuart Fisher and Denis Maloney, who could clearly see the motivational value to the school.

Then they opened up the engine that had set the record. "It was in terrible shape", said Appleby. "There are about 255 blades in the compressor, and each of those is individually replaceable. At least 50% of those needed either replacing or reworking. On top of that the compressor casing was quite worn - it actually had pits in it - and wasn't creating the right flow path. The whole engine was performing way below its proper efficiency". (This, of course, was engine No.3. No.1 had been cooked when Warby hit a beer can and water flooded into the intakes, No.2 by the screwdriver disaster; No.3 was the rusting old bugger of a thing lying under the tree in Concord).

Said Appleby: "We'd heard things through the RAAF grapevine about Warby.....most of them bad, in that he was out to use the RAAF and was a scrounger with the wild idea and no money out to get what he could. I'd met him a couple of times and couldn't reconcile that with the man I'd met". The RAAF assumed the responsibility not only of servicing the engines but also the boat. "I decided we had to get it on a professional level, so I called Ken into the office and said this had to be done the RAAF way. We would open-up documentation on the boat as with any aircraft and document the lot with a servicing schedule so the apprentices could learn. We would set the parameters of test runs in terms of engine revs-per-minute (rpm). His reply was: 'Well, if that's the way the professionals do it, then that's the way we do it.' That changed my opinion of the man".

Apart from the engine, the RAAF team found about 30 things wrong with the boat itself, like the way the steering column was mounted and the steering connected to the rudder via a piece of welding rod instead of a split pin. They recalibrated all the gauges as well. "The boat at this stage was four to five years old and getting a bit tired, so we went over it with a fine-toothed comb", said Appleby. "Most of the work was done out of hours, at night. We couldn't make them work out of hours, but when we asked for volunteers, we were swamped". On the first test at Blowering Warby got to 180mph (290km/h) before he knew it, but Appleby's team re-wrote their servicing schedules because of changes they had found in the boat due to trailering between Wagga and Blowering - about 200 kilometres. (For the record, the apprentice members of the team were named John Blackadder, Russell Harris, John Davison, Denis Hibbs, Shane Davis, Les Haddon and Paul Cahill). "All we did was what we had been trained to do on aircraft", Appleby would say years later.

Warby's long-time friend, film-maker McCauley, who had come back from an assignment in Papua-New Guinea with a bad bout of dengue fever, wasn't sure it was all good. "It had become a whole different ball game......like a military exercise. Ken was no longer the builder, the mechanic who was busy-busy-busy until the time came to pull on the helmet. It worried me because here he was walking around with nothing to do. I took Appleby aside and asked him to leave some things undone, so Ken could pick up a spanner. So they gave him the job of doing the final checks. But it was quite a different scene from that first time".

McCauley was worried that Warby was becoming a sort of Evel Knievel, a circus performer. He was also getting annoyed at the quotes he was seeing from Warby in the media. "I've spoken to him about it a lot. You couldn't call Ken a whinger — not for one moment.....not in the normal sense.....but I've got fairly cranky with him through the years by him continually getting the feeling Australia didn't do enough for him and the public didn't do enough for him. It's got to the stage of saying perhaps the reason you find it difficult getting sponsors is the fact you've had a press where you've said Australia doesn't give a damn about you, and from where I'm standing there's a headline. He found great difficulty in accepting this and told the press I've done this for King and country, next time it will be for dollars......what Campbell received in Australia, like the Army support and the rest, was good reason for Warby to be disappointed. But he didn't do too badly in areas allowing the funding of a small group of people who helped him make his mark".

None of that mattered now. For what was coming up was the demon - the attempt by a boat driver to raise their own record, and which had always killed them.......

"Bloody Bumpy Through That Kilo"

McCauley, like Warby, was baffled by the lack of interest Australians showed in the record. He recut all the ABC footage (at Warby's expense) into a second, hour-long documentary called "The Fastest Man In The World On Water". But while it was sold to more than 30 countries, no Australian TV channel would look at it. "We were talking with a Channel 10 marketing guy called Cleary, and he said: 'Look, to be quite frank with you Ken, yes, what you did was bloody marvellous, but to be quite frank with you I don't think the people of Australia are interested one bit'. It was incredibly blunt, unpleasant way of saying to Ken: 'Oh look, piss off, we're not going to buy your story because no-one's interested in what you did'. Ken walked out saying: 'Aw, fuck him, what would he know......'

"One aspect I've never understood about the Warby image....try as we could, and through lots of personal contacts and business contacts, we were never able to succeed in getting Warby a big endorsement, such as a TV personality endorsing product. I can't understand why having used Shell oil and Shell fuel for his record attempts and with such an incredibly visible object such as Spirit Shell didn't have those big posters at service stations and the rest". McCauley was able to make six five-minute films for Film Australia on safer boating using Warby as presenter. Ken enrolled on the celebrity speaker circuit but although he is a consummate speaker, displaying lots of warmth and charm, he got hardly a booking, where an ageing Channel swimmer called Des Renford (also a great speaker) was in constant demand.

Shell's special duties retail manager in head office, Cyril Arnold, had contracted Warby originally through the company's long-time motor sport manager, Archie White. (Shell paid for Warby to go to Lewisham Hospital's top-rank sporting medical unit for physical and mental testing, and he passed with flying colors). "Ken felt that when he got the world record he would become an instant millionaire", Arnold said. "But he wasn't an easy bloke to sponsor because he was using oil products not of great interest to the general public — the fuel was jet fuel, the oils were specific to jet engines. The product marketing just wasn't there". Shell gave him a credit card for all fuel and oil, not just for Spirit but for all the support boats, and picked up much of his accommodation bills.

But to Warby, it was nothing like the commitment Shell's biggest rival, BP, had given Donald Campbell. Eighteen years after setting that first world record he was still bitter. "Campbell had a habit in Australia of charging everything to Bluebird, but Bluebird never had a bloody bank account. There were a lot of unpaid bills left behind. The whole Campbell episode (the world land speed record on Lake Eyre) was involved in horsehit. He really went through millions and millions. I think originally his father had the money and the ability and the style to carry it off. Donald didn't have the money, but he had a lot of his father's camp followers and tried to live in the style of his father......a lot of media-grabbing bullshit. One wonders how much of Campbell was for real. I admire the guy for his guts, but there were reports from the journalists at Lake Eyre that the world was waiting for him to have a run and he's saying the conditions weren't right, but some journos claimed he was holding-out because he was being paid by the day by BP."

Warby quietly slipped in to Hume's Crossing at Blowering on September 17, Spirit with its rebuilt engine and in its new livery, bearing the names of Speedo, Shell and Channel Ten. He had named the weekend of October 7-8 for the next record attempt, but had learned his lessons and was doing the testing without much media fanfare. He was running without an afterburner, although a second engine back at the RAAF base was fitted with one, the technicians finally discovering that the wrong part sent from the US was the reason for the continuing failures. Warby ran the boat in both directions, getting up to around 275mph (442.5km/h) before an under-tensioned clamp allowed burning gas to escape. At the same time a bearing failed in the turbine. But the run established that the boat now had 200 pounds of thrust over standard where before it was 800 pounds under, and Warby didn't find it hard to agree with Tom Fink, who opposed the use of the afterburner "unless absolutely necessary".

On the Friday night of the big weekend, the Tumut RSL Club staged a testimonial dinner for Warby and the media, the highlight a sculptured margarine model of Spirit. Almost 100 media people were in Tumut, and in a speech Bob Apathy reminded the audience that when the record went down for the first time "we got a story on page 13 of the *Sydney Morning Herald* and page 14 of the *West Australian*". The RSL club president, a rotund gent called Charles O'Brien, led everyone in a rousing chorus of "Glory, glory to Ken Warby", sung to the tune of "The Battle Hymn Of The Republic".

Out at Blowering they were dragging the lake with a long shallow net to clear it of snags and debris. But when Warby arrived at the dam at 6am on the Saturday the water was far from clean, and Apathy organised an armada of 10 boats armed with lengths of chicken wire. As well, the wind had got up and there was a nasty chop of around 25 centimetres. Warby didn't get out until 12.20, and he ran down the first leg at 297.9mph (479.3km/h). Refuelling at the other end, the timekeepers gave him an estimate that 305 would be needed on the return. Over the two-way radio Apathy was worrying at him. Warby said: "Bumpy - bloody bumpy through that kilo, old buddy". Apathy: "Before you hop in that cockpit how about we have a chat about it?" Warby: "I'm already in there — I'll be careful". But it nearly killed him.

For 1978 the RAAF approved using Warby's jet engines as a training ground for apprentices. Led by Group Captain Bob Bartram (right) it was a huge win.

The old hat over the eyes trick; KW relaxes as they wait for smooth water for the Big One – upping the record again, and the first through 300 mph.

Despite the first world record, the Blowering "boaties" were still aggro the next year. This was yet another Chamber of Commerce meeting to sort it.

Mark Spencer, editor of the prestigious US Powerboat *magazine, flew in for the second record runs. He backed Warby totally despite US jealousy.*

The Challenge Cup, the world water speed record trophy, which took 18 months and diplomatic channels to wrest from Lee Taylor's jealous grip.

A now white-haired father Neville with son Ken during a 1987 whistle-stop Australian tour. After a few disagreements, they had made their peace.

Qantas regional director, John Rowe, presents KW with the Challenge Cup. But Qantas refused financial recognition for his use of "Spirit of Australia".

In 1979 came Roger Climpson and "This Is Your Life". Evelyn embraces her boy as grandson David looks on, watched by the RAAF's Bob Bartram.

On March 12, 1980, Spirit was given rare permission for a 300 km/h demonstration run on Lake Burley Griffin in the national capital, Canberra.

Warby's three sons. L to R: Peter, David and Michael. Warby hoped that Peter or David might co-drive the new boat he was to design in America.

On the set of "This Is Your Life", KW with the RAAF crew that won him 1978. On his left. Professor Tom Fink, and next to him Dave Appleby.

In 1980 the Warby circus started a five-month, 39-state US tour with the boat, with a Chevrolet wagon towing the trailered Spirit and a motorhome.

On his US tour in Minneapolis – where he would shortly settle – Warby met actor Claude Atkins, who had played the television role of Sheriff Lobo.

During trials for match races with France III for the 1980 America's Cup shoot-out, skipper Jim Hardy handed the tiller to a guest steerer – KW.

With Spirit retired to the Sydney Maritime Museum, Warby turned to jet-powered dragsters, an easy move, given his total familiarity with the engines.

From jet dragsters was a small step to jet "funny cars" and several tours with Sue Ransom, one of Australia's best female race drivers of the 1970s-80s.

Warby bought two jet funny cars from Craig Arfons. As "Thunderman" and "Thunderwoman", the show toured the US, Australia and the West Indies.

Warby's "Thunder From Downunder" tour broke attendance records everywhere they toured. In 1987-88. Warby even ran a Mustang convertible.

Ravenswood (Perth) Dragway, 1987, and flames erupt from the exhaust stacks of the Ford Louisville jet truck as Warby lights up for a seven-second quarter.

American Tom Brown (right) retired after being fearfully burned in a jet car explosion. Here he watches KW accept a trophy for a US-Aussie challenge.

Warby retired after Tom Brown's crash and started his Mini-Mix business in the US, capitalising on the lack of small trucks for homeowner concrete pours.

In 1996 Warby started designing a new boat, also made of wood, with some carbon-fibre, powered by a Westinghouse J34 engine developing 9000 hp.

The final version of Spirit II made its public debut in the US in January, 2000. Warby planned to attack the record again at his old home of Blowering Dam.

Warby wets the new boat for the first time, sticking to his past with a low-speed run at the Aquatic Carnival in Taree's Manning River, January, 2005.

The new boat, named "Aussie Spirit", did another demo at Taree in June, 2005. But the long Australian drought ruined all venues for record-chasing.

Back with "Aussie Spirit" in the US, Warby hooked up with the AMF Off-Shore Racing Team as patron. He even had AMF sponsorship on the boat.

The last shot "Aussie Spirit II" fired in anger, on October 16, 2007. On November 20 he announced his retirement – appropriately exactly 20 years on.

A model of "American Challenge", the technology-packed fighter-like boat Russ Wicks claims will set the new record. Warby doesn't think much of it.

"Quicksilver" in digitalised art model form, the boat in which Britisher Michael Macknight claims he will attack Warby's record some time in 2010.

And what really started Warby on his quest. Diver Bill Smith sits atop the wreckage of Campbell's Bluebird he recovered from Coniston in 2001.

Restoration of Campbell's Bluebird is now almost complete. It is destined for a Campbell museum established in 2009 at Coniston Water.

"I was fine until I hit the rough area in the timing zone. It was full of white-tops and the boat buffetted and shook and generally danced all over the place. I got two or three feet in the air for a couple of hundred feet and I remember hitting down on one of the bounces and I slipped forward in the seat and my backside was under the wheel and my head was where my backside should have been and I was looking at the sky. My knees were jammed under the screen but luckily my foot slipped off the power. The boat took a long time to slow down". Apathy later estimated that Spirit flew for 200 metres about 60cm off the surface. The bashing had been so severe that two bolts in the taiplane mounting had sheared and the right-hand fuel tank had split.

Repairing the latter would mean cutting-out the deck, so Warby decided to blank-off that tank. Full tanks weigh 136 kilograms each side, so without one Spirit would be out of balance, but because the engine torque twisted the boat against the left weighting it wouldn't be so bad. "We decided to cross our fingers for tomorrow and hope", Warby said. He got back to the caravan to find that son Peter — whom Warby had brought to Blowering for the first time — had appropriated his sleeping bag, so he sat around the campfire talking and drinking coffee until 3am and woke with pains from a chill in the kidneys.

They were ready to go at 9am but once again there was a delay in setting-up the timing gear. The officials estimated a two-hour wait, so Warby lay down on a fender of the boat trailer, pulled his battered Akubra hat over his face and went to sleep. "When they woke me and said we're ready to go I threw away my hat and put my helmet on. The start boat came alongside, plugged in and I fired up. I went down to the dam wall end of the lake, the northern end. I did a U-turn, lined up the Yellowfin Bay entrance to the southern end of the lake, put my foot down, and let her go". He had left behind, sobbing against the tailgate of a station wagon and refusing to look at the water, his 69-year-old mother Sal.

"The water was good....probably about a 3-4-inch chop, probably the best I'd had. I just sat there and let the boat take me. It was a fairly effortless ride, although the boat was skidding around a little bit. When I pulled up at the other end I radioed back to Bob for the speed and they confirmed it was over 300". They were talking in code because some of the press were on the same CB channel. "Zero Mark" was 300, so the code as "Plus Five" or "Minus 10" or whatever. Warby had told the crew he didn't want to run higher than a 310mph (498km/h) two-way average because he wanted to save the 500 km/h mark for the next year. Author Tuckey was there at the turnaround.

Refuelling saw them nearly 20% short of maximum capacity in that left tank, because an air lock had sucked fuel away from the pickup, so they had to bleed the fuel system. They were getting close to the end of the hour in which he had to make the return run. But they got it started, as the rich red flame blossomed a full metre from the tailpipe and then the whine started and the huge rooster tail started to grow and the banshee scream was echoing around the hot dry hills, Warby couldn't help himself. He decided to give the throttle "a bit of a nudge" to see how the boat would handle for next year. "I hit it one and a half seconds too early and it accelerated like all hell and went to 350 very quickly. So we would end up with more than 310". From the small hill where most of the media had set up, the beautiful white arrow, rocking gently from side to side, was so quick that photographers had no time to change the focal length of their lenses.

In the crash boat that came to tow him in was John Sutton of the St George Motor Boat Club. Warby handed him the brown handkerchief he had borrowed to clean his goggles and visor just before the start. Sutton had said to him: "Just bring it back dry". "Here you are", said Warby; "the fastest handkerchief in the world". As they eased into the ramp Warby yelled: "Lee Taylor, eat your heart out". Red pressure-suited, shaggy-bearded, sweaty, he stepped ashore to embrace his mother, who was shaking and crying. "You'll finish now?" she said, as the media cameras crowd in. "No more?" All Warby could say was: "Come on Sal, we'll talk about it later". Aside to the microphones he said: "She said that about my first boat, and it would do only 25 mph. How are you, you bloody old scene-stealer?" The RAAF team, in blue tracksuits Warby had bought for them, were dancing around singing: "Hooray for Kenneth, hooray at last; hooray for Kenneth, he's the horse's arse". Up came the staff from the Tumut Oriental Hotel bearing the Methuselah of sparkling wine they had promised him. But they had to wait almost an hour before the average speed came out — 317.186 mph (510.452 km/h). He had broken the record by 29 mph, the largest margin in the record's history, and had been the first to go through the

300 barrier and lived to tell the tale. It would be upped slightly after official revision.

The questions came thick and fast — could the boat go faster, when would he try to lift the record again, would he fit the afterburner......Warby reminded them that he had promised Professor Fink he wouldn't take the boat over 350 mph (563km/h). "Spirit could do 450 but it never will", he said. Would he build another one? Maybe.

This time he made the front pages big-time of every major Australian metropolitan newspaper, as well as that night's TV news. They had to get the boat back to Sydney and clean it up, because it was scheduled to go on display in the centre of the city the next day. On the trip north the truckies were all over him on the CB, blasting their air horns as they flashed past. The next morning the media were calling from all over the world, and at the Australia Square display in the city Warby was mobbed. Channel Seven ambushed him and surprised him with "This Is Your Life". It was all very different to a year ago. But one Sydney journalist wrote that the achievement was about as important as an airline captain breaking the Sydney-Melbourne flight record.

Of Lee Taylor's Sour Grapes

Warby had started to plan a 12-months tour of Australia with the boat, a shopping centre whistle-stop that would give him income for perhaps 12 months, with backing from Speedo and Shell. But he was starting to think seriously about going overseas, this time not because of his neglect by the Australian media but because of what had started appearing in international media days and weeks after the record run. Mark Spencer, editor of the prestigious US *Powerboat* magazine, had been at Blowering for the second record — his air tickets had been provided by the Australian Government. He had written a glittering tale about the achievement, as well as cementing a friendship with Warby with a promise to open some doors in the US. In Warby's four huge meticulously-kept scrapbooks there are stories from South Africa's *Yachting* magazine, *Powerboat Waterskiing* and *Motorboat And Yachting* in the UK, in Germany *Jobby* and *Badynt* magazines, in France *Neptune Nautisme*, *Les Cahiers*

Du Yachting ("500 km/h sur l'eau!" the headline trumpeted); in newspapers and magazines in Singapore, Fiji, New Zealand, Thailand, Indonesia, Borneo, The Philippines, Russia, China, Malaysia.......

In his between-records trip to Britain and the US Warby had met Leo Villa, who asked him when he would get the trophy. Warby said: "What trophy?" He had never heard of the Challenge Cup, the King George V silver, but soon found out Lee Taylor had it. Through Mark Spencer he then met Taylor in the offices of *Power Boating* magazine in Van Nuys in the US. Warby: "From the time he walked into the office to the time he walked out Taylor did nothing but quiz me and quiz me. He never mentioned the trophy. Indeed, I found out later he had sent to the international body for photostats of all my paperwork and timing sheets and gave them to a mathematician to try and prove my record wrong. He didn't want to believe I had broken it with such a simple boat with less thrust than his and no money."

It would take Warby 18 months and extensive excuses by Taylor for Warby to get the trophy — and then only after using diplomatic channels. Taylor finally handed it to the Australian Consul-General in Los Angeles, Peter Barbour, in the first week of April, 1979, saying "Tell Ken to take good care of it. I'll be coming to Australia fairly soon to bring it back home". Qantas flew the Challenge Cup to Australia and handed it to Warby on April 20, 1979.

"He was a very strange fellow", Warby would say later. "I didn't have much respect for the guy at all". For a moment let us fast-forward to June, 1980, when Warby was again in the US doing a promotion tour with Spirit and Taylor, 45, was testing his new 15-metre-long aluminium rocket-powered hydrogen-peroxide-fuelled "US Discovery II" on Walker Lake in Nevada. He had claimed to the press he had hit 343 mph(552km/h) in preliminary testing but Warby had commissioned a security firm to monitor it and says this was "bullshit".

Taylor had already had one bad crash when he flipped over a sandbank and the helicopter that was lifting him had crashed on top of him. "People who knew him said that changed him and affected him mentally", said Warby. "He had trouble keeping his people together. They said he was difficult to work with. He was putting out dummy figures not just to get press but to put pressure on himself. Taylor eventually found out I was spying on him — he could have come down and watched everything I had done in my runs and it wouldn't have worried me — and he was furious. I told him any more dummy figures and I would nail him, because I had the evidence. That stopped him".

On November 6, 1980, a week before he was to make his record attempt, Taylor arrived at the Buena Park shopping mall in Orange County (California), where Spirit was on display. "He proceeded to tell me what a heap of shit my boat was and what he was going to do, and that I should keep the packaging the trophy came in because it would be needed very soon. He invited me down to Lake Tahoe but I said I didn't want to go and see him killed. I had told several of his people his boat was badly designed and would bounce in the wrong conditions. It was obvious it was flexing.....it had a whole heap of problems. In his final test runs he couldn't get over 186mph (300km/h) and the boat buckled in the middle. They riveted-in aluminium panels to stiffen it and pumped pressure into the rocket like it had never seen before". Warby told him the sponsons were set at the wrong angle and would cause the boat to flip over.

In January, 1979, the media had fastened onto a story that an American entrepreneur was arranging a $1 million match race in the US between Warby and Taylor's boat, now owned by a syndicate and renamed Crazy Man, but it was never on. On November 12, 1980, Lee Taylor put into the Lake Tahoe water for his revenge-on-Warby boat that looked like a long slim pencil sitting on water skis. Designed by aero engineer Art Williams with little experience of fluid dynamics, it had reputedly cost $US2.25 million. "It was probably the most expensive coffin in history", Warby says now.

Taylor was strapped into a sealed cockpit with full harness; the concept was that if the boat did crash, he would survive in the safety cell. With 8500 pounds of thrust squirting out through a 10cm hole, the boat started to slew sideways at a reported 418 km/h. It began to break up, but observers said the cockpit seemed to fly through the debris in one piece. All that came to the surface was Taylor's helmet, lightly scratched.

The Challenge Cup went on display at the St George Motor Boat Club in Sydney, the only club, said Warby, that had given him any help, which was unfair, because the Wagga Boat Club had slaved for him at Blowering. Warby was collecting the awards from all kinds of organisations, including his home town of Newcastle, at club gatherings, a children's day at the Wagga RAAF base, with most things timed to coincide with the shopping centre appearances. On March 12, 1980, Spirit of Australia wetted its hull again, this time on the precious Lake Burley Griffin that bisects the national capital of Canberra and which is now totally banned to all power boats but at that time restricted them to eight knots. Somehow the organisers got permission and he ran bridge to bridge in the centre of the lake in front of the old Parliament House in 22 seconds — about 200mph (320km/h).

By May the story had broken that Warby was designing a new boat, aiming for 600 km/h-plus. Warby had in fact sketched just such a boat, a tandem two-seater catamaran type looking like a pickle fork, and in his spare time was building a model. But by then he was on a six-weeks publicity tour of Europe and the US, including that eerie visit to Coniston Water to lay wreaths on the spot where Donald Campbell had died. By August he was in Perth for the big boat show and listed to run Spirit for the second last time, down the Swan River that bisects the city. Before the run he told the press: "Doing 320 km/h down the Swan will be like a Saturday morning drive. Which it will be". It wasn't. Afterwards a shaken Warby said: "That's the closest I have ever come to death".

What happened was that with the run starting from a place called The Narrows the public had been told to have all their boats in designated anchoring areas by 10am. Warby cranked it up to around 200mph (320km/h) and then slowed to 40mph (60km/h) under the Narrows Bridge, as requested, and then found himself with a good long run back to the yacht club, so he floored it. "What I didn't know was that there was a cruiser with a camera crew on board who decided they wanted a different camera angle and they crossed over at a speed which meant they dug some nice big holes in the water. I hit the rollers at close to 200 mph and I figure I flew more than 100 metres before I came down again and skipped a couple of times". The crash broke loose the fire extinguisher and Warby went up out of his seat and slammed down on his spine, bruising himself so badly he couldn't walk properly for a week. "I remember flying through the air and thinking: 'Who was the dumb bastard who did this?'".

By January, 1980, Warby was confirmed to be headed for the US on an Australian Government-funded promotional tour."I'm going overseas to do some bragging", he told John Waugh of *Sundowner* magazine. "I've got some beaut film footage of Australian technology in action, such as over-the-horizon radar and our giant mining operations, which are the best in the world. That's the sort of image I'm going to push in America — not for me, but for all Australians". The man the government had just appointed as a member of the committee organising the national day, Australia Day, had some advice for his fellow Aussies: "I'd just tell them simply to get off their backsides and do something. I don't care what they do, but whatever they do they should try to be the best. They've got the ability and the courage but many of them waste it". The ideas of taking the boat to Russia and the UK had been dropped. Instead, Spirit was to be taken on the American tour, the taxpayers to pick up much of the $200,000 bill.

But by February, 1980, Dave Appleby, now Squadron-Leader, and the RAAF apprentices were refurbishing the boat — with the afterburner engine — for what Warby was saying would be another attack on the record, scheduling it for Blowering on April 12-13. He announced a target of 325mph (523km/h), saying he had again promised not to go over 350mph (563km/h). But a continuing drought had been dropping the Blowering water level, and by early April, when the run length had effectively been cut by three kilometres, Warby had to call it off. He headed for the US and a schedule that called for Spirit to do the usual shopping mall appearances, and the Newport Boat Show. But the hull would never kiss water again. The Spirit of Australia was destined for the National Maritime Museum at Darling Harbour in Sydney, and Warby was on the verge of deciding to desert Australia and live in the US.....

Thunder From Downunder

Five months and 39 states in his US tour had started to firm-up Warby's plans for the future. He had been offered $100,000 to run the boat in the US with a sponsor's name replacing Spirit of Australia, but had knocked it back. "If I'd lived in America I'd certainly have a lot more money than I've got now". But a meeting with veteran jet drag racer Romeo Palamides gave him the idea of using one of his J34 engines in a drag car, doing exhibition runs for appearance money. That grew into the concept of running two cars, one in American colours, one Australian, in match racing around Australia and possibly the US, thus generating the cash to build the next boat, target 400mph (644km/h).

Palamides had built two jet dragsters for American gun Tom Brown, so with two engines doing nothing Warby ordered two chassis at a cost of around US$14,000 each. With sponsorship from Speedo and Winfield cigarettes, Warby's "Advance Australia" and Brown's "US Invader" by

January 3, 1981 had started touring Australia with what was billed as the "Winfield World Series". The cars weren't all that rapid by today's standards, running the quarter-mile in around seven seconds with a terminal speed of about 370 km/h, but the pyrotechnics were awesome, particularly at night, and drew huge crowds to see the first jet dragsters to run in Australia.

"The speed isn't a problem", said Warby, always the master of the 10-second sound grab. "You've got time to smell the flowers in these". Warby says the US National Hot Rod Association (NHRA), which controls drag racing in America, always hated jet cars and would fine and then suspend the drivers for getting to within 10mph of the wheel-driven AA fuellers.

There was a fair bit of showbiz in the series, of course. The jet cars were far cheaper to run than the Top Fuel dragsters, because they didn't blow engines or use-up parts, other than brakes and tyres. Warby was so familiar with jets the transition was almost seamless. The procedure was to crank the electric starter for 10-12 seconds, and once fired, the J34 Westinghouse would idle at 55% power. Warby would then dump afterburner fuel into the hot exhaust gases in the tailpipe which would turn the kerosene first into smoke and then into a huge fireball. Then he would roll to the staging line, taking the engine up to 95% with the brakes on hard and switching the afterburner on and off, producing more spectacle. As the "Christmas Tree" countdown of starting lights began he would shut the bleed doors and go to full power. On the last yellow light before the green he would hit the afterburner button and drop the foot off the brakes.

Because the cars ran on thrust they seldom tried to kill the driver, unlike the long, vicious, nitromethane-burning 1600-horsepower fuel dragsters. Did he get a buzz driving these cars? "Oh, it did at times. Sometimes it got mundane, sometimes I felt I was just going through the same routine week in week out. It became a job more than a sport". The circus did three 10-week tours of Australia, and then headed for the US.

But his life was changing dramatically. His mother, Sal, had a stroke late in 1980 and another one in 1981. Hospitalised with pneumonia, she had a heart attack just after Christmas and died a week later. His marriage to Jan was coming apart, not so much because of his absences and his unwillingness - inherited from his father - to share-out his emotions but also probably because Jan was getting tired of his philandering. Long-time family friend Daphne Lynch says Jan was "dead against going to America. I think she was a bit frightened of it". To this day Warby won't expand much on the reasons for the divorce except to say: "It was a gradual disintegration over a very long time. It would probably have been more beneficial to the marriage had she stood by my side. We sort of drifted apart and I became much more of a loner. She turned within herself. There was no big fight or anything like that. I tried to make things easier for her in the divorce but she was just terribly bloody stubborn". They separated in October, 1982.

One of his closest friends said later Warby had long ago built a veneer around himself to stop emotion intruding.

When things were going wrong, whether it was with the boat or a personal relationship, he would shrug and say: "She'll be right" and get on with doing something else. "He's a totally selfish man in the true sense of the world. He didn't appear to have a close relationship with his kids, possibly because he was never there to discipline them - to the point where he was able to walk out on Jan and the kids and go to the US to start a new life. There's only a small degree of responsibility there".

And then there were the other women. While Warby cared little about clothes, this big, shaggy, bear of a man seemed to have some subliminal animal smell about him that drew women like starving seagulls around a wounded prawn. Said the same friend: "It got to the stage where he was almost bragging....it was sort of juvenile the way he talked about the ladies he'd had and how he used to get away with things".

Rob McCauley tells a story about how a Newcastle friend had come to Concord in Sydney to visit and he and Ken had gone out on the town, picked up two women, and crawled in around three in the morning. In the morning Jan said to them: 'Where were you last night?' and Ken said: 'All right, I'll tell you where we were. We were with two blondes up at Kings Cross and we had dinner and afterwards we went home and me mate and I we fucked them to death', and Jan said: 'Oh, don't be ridiculous Ken - who'd have you? Where did you really go last night?' And he said his friend from Newcastle, when he was telling Jan exactly what they had done, sat there with his mouth open, terrified about what was going to happen. "Jan must have been fairly naive about Ken's extra-curricular activities because I've got a feeling there was a lot of them".

There was only one semi-permanent mistress, as far as this author's research has gone. She was a stunningly-beautiful woman with a great personality, married and living with two children in Canberra, which was conveniently on the road from Sydney down to Tumut and Blowering Dam. She even took her husband and children down to Blowering for a few of the record attempts. One friend said: "The husband must have been as stupid as hell because it was obvious there was total magic between those two. It was a very physical relationship because he talked fairly animal about her, how they had it off in the most extraordinary situations, like on the bonnet of the car just out of town one night". Her marriage crashed into divorce and she moved to Sydney to live but typically, Warby didn't want it when it was easy to get and went back out hunting.

Warby ran the two jet dragsters in Australia and the US for about a year. He made a lot of money, and when the word came through that the NHRA had sanctioned jet-engined "funny cars" he decided to get in on the ground floor. He bought two that had just been built by Craig Arfons, whose father Art had briefly held the world land speed record in an ugly tank called "The Green Monster". A funny car is a fibreglass shell with the styling of a street car — in this case one a Nissan 280Z, the other a 1982 Ford Mustang — over a dragster chassis of chrome-molybdenum steel tube. The jet engines were General Electric J85s out of Northrop F5 fighters.

Warby broke attendance records everywhere he went with the cars, and when Sue Ransom, arguably Australia's best-ever female race driver, told him she wanted to make the transition from driving an alcohol fueller to the jet cars Warby created "Thunderwoman". He became "Thunderman". The two of them - and it was as far as the author knows, a partnership, a platonic friendship - took the show around Australia and all over the US and the West Indies, campaigning as "Thunder From Downunder", with good sponsorship from the big Australian Repco parts maker. They pulled enormous crowds, won national jet drag championship titles and set new speed records, their normal "pass" over the quarter-mile about six seconds with a terminal speed of 260mph (418km/h). But to Warby it was boring, nowhere near as dangerous or as challenging as the boat.

"At the end of 1987 I said to myself, this is stupid", Warby would say in 1993. "When I started there were 10 jet cars in the US; when I sold out there were about 70". So he switched to jet trucks. Few things more bizarre have ever existed. Built in Michigan by one Fred Sibley and raced briefly by Billy McDaniels and Rick Roxburgh, Warby's new toy was rebuilt by Craig Arfons to Warby's specifications. What was created was a Ford Louisville LTL9000 with a J79 jet out of an F4 Phantom fighter or B52 bomber. Its 18,000 pounds of thrust would hurl the four-tonne behemoth over a quarter-mile in around seven seconds with a terminal speed of 210mph (338km/h). He brought the truck to Australia to tour it with the cars. "It was like driving a brick shithouse", he said later. "I had two six-metre parachutes and four-spot NASCAR disc brakes but I ran out of track a lot of times doing three runs a night, sometimes ending sideways against a steel fence".

He decided to give it away not long after his friend Tom Brown was fearfully burned in an engine explosion in his own car at Cayuga in Canada in September, 1992. He survived, despite third-degree burns over 50% of his body. Warby's second wife, American-born Sandy (nee Powell), had "been at me a long time to get a real job". Her father was in the business of delivering concrete by truck, and Warby had for a while been toying with the idea of introducing the US to the Mini-Mix concept. Uniquely Australian, this was a two or three-cubic-yard concrete pourer mounted on a small Daihatsu cab-chassis. The Americans laughed at the idea, but Warby built his concrete plant in Cincinatti himself and started canvassing project home builders and existing home owners as a small load contractor. What the big American concrete firms called "cocktail mixers" clicked, and Warby was finished with the jets - boats or cars or trucks....

That is, until 1996.........

New Boat, New Rivals

In 1996, during a trip back to Australia with his third partner – his second marriage had also failed – Ken Warby told author Tuckey that he had started building a new boat in his Cincinatti (Ohio) garage. This one would run an afterburner and have significantly more "grunt", he said. Two years later, on another visit, Tuckey arranged for him to meet with the Victorian State Government's Major Events Committee, headed by the influential Ron Walker, who had gained the Australian Formula One Grand Prix for Albert Park. The basis of the meeting was that Warby would go for a new record with the new boat on central Victoria's Lake Eildon instead of the Blowering Dam in NSW. Melbourne television station GTV-9 flew him to Eildon in its chopper, and Warby came back impressed by the fact that Eildon offered a lot more length, better spectator facilities and the assurance of the government that it would put whatever it could at his disposal. Tuckey even set up with Holden an initial agreement to supply Warby with vehicles as ground transport, including a towmaster for the trailer.

But Warby, typically, trusted only the things he had proved to work. He resisted the idea of Eildon. As well, he was designing the new boat on almost exactly the same lines as the Spirit of Australia. He even went to the extent of sounding-out (former) Major Bob Apathy to run the logistics for a new attempt. He had become disillusioned with his first son Peter – for reasons that aren't relevant to this book – and said his son David, who was sharing his time between Australia and his father in the US, and who had started racing boats, might well drive the new device. "He has the fire".

The son of the man with the fastest wooden boat on water, David had at the 1998 Wooden Boat Show met up with Jim Broadley, the owner of Diablo Motors, who owned "Diablo" – built and named "Jag" in 1955 - that Ken had raced against in his Newcastle circuit racing days. David Warby got Diablo out of the shed and started restoring it, re-laying the plywood deck, refurbishing the hull and fitting a new V8 engine. He later moved to a new circuit racing hydroplane called "Aussie Spirit".

Meanwhile, his recalcitrant father was well down the old familiar path. Drawing-up the new boat by himself, he again placed his faith in wood. The timber body that took shape in the Cincinatti garage was in essence a flat-floored and flat-backed shape with two huge pointed and multi-compartmented sponsons running down to the front. In the back, shrouded in carbon-fibre (the first time Warby had used this material to any degrees) was a J34-WE-34 Westinghouse jet engine with an afterburner (the failure of the afterburner on the Spirit had, it was later found, been due to the wrong specifications sent from the US and in any case, Warby by now was totally comfortable with the technology because of his jet cars and trucks).

The J34 engine dates back to the late 1940s, replacing the J30, and was used in several experimental US Air Force (USAF) aircraft up to 1953. Again, it was Warby stubbornly staying in his comfort zone, because it was a replica of the engine used in the Spirit, although of a later series. With an afterburner it would develop 5000 pounds of thrust, which computes to 9000 horsepower against the 6000 horsepower in the Spirit. Warby claims the engine cost him US$68,000, but that seems fairly excessive for an engine no longer useful in anything except car and boat racing.

The new boat looks like the Spirit reincarnated, except it has a full cockpit canopy. While it is 44 centimetres longer, at 868cm, it has the same long, pointed nose, big side sponsons, twin air intakes astride the cockpit, and the tailplane, albeit set a little lower. Even the cockpit is similar down to the drilled-spoke steering wheel and red seat trim, the main difference a large red button on the wheel to fire the afterburner. The gauges are the "air speedo" (pitot), exhaust gas temperature, rev counter (properly the percent gauge), engine oil pressure, afterburner fuel pressure, and a bank of switches for various functions – all familiar.

Warby's web site claims the boat was "pronounced complete on December 23, 1999". But the old nemesis returned; Warby still had to raise the sponsorship money, and his web site in May, 2003, in announcing the boat would be "unveiled" at the Australian National Maritime

Museum in Sydney's Darling Harbour (where the Spirit lives) on October 8, was still calling for sponsor interest, despite claiming negotiations were under way with a potential boat-naming sponsor.

It was Warby all over again. The new boat actually made its public debut on January 14, 2000, at the Cincinatti Travel, Sports and Boat Show. The Australian Embassy in Washington, DC, issued a statement of congratulations, saying the new challenge was scheduled for 2001. The PR bumpf also quoted Warby as saying: "I'm launching my new boat in the US to ensure it draws more attention and exposure throughout not only North America, but internationally as well". Once again, he was talking-up things early.

By September 2000 the boat was being displayed on its six-wheel trailer, it and the towmaster sign-written with the Warby name. But more than two years later it was still unsponsored. When Warby finally announced his intention of breaking his own record again, he said it was "most likely" the boat would run at Blowering Dam and the attempt would again be managed by Bob Apathy. His web site in May, 2003, said: "Ken, at the frisky age of 64, is about breaking his record. He thinks that 24 years is too long for a record to stand, and is plenty of time for all the 'Gunnas' of the world to do something about breaking the record".

The "Gunnas" – a unique Australian word describing those who keep saying they're "going to" do something – was aimed at three potential rivals. One was the oddly-named "Southern Cross Water Shuttle", built for a

Sydney-based Australian, Kevin Hickling. With styling that owed a lot to Spirit, it was sponsored by a firm called "Aussie-Life". Hickling's main claim to fame was that in 1986 he set the "world alternate fuel water speed record" – which still stands – at 182.9 km/h. The boat ran a formidable supercharged 7.2-litre Chevrolet V8 developing about 600 kW in an Australian-designed "pickle-fork" type of hull.

Warby, never averse to criticising potential rivals and seasoned by many years of experience with the bitchy membership of speedboat clubs, approved his web site's statement that the Hickling boat "has been around for 15 years and (sic) made many absurd speed claims, but he won't put the boat through the clocks......Ken's belief is that it will 'back-flip' before 300mph. Ken also wonders what record this 'record-breaking boat' set. Certainly nothing has been recorded with the Australian Power Boat Association. Maybe it is just another 'Gunna' record or maybe the fastest boat on a trailer going to the lake". And in his own words: "It's time he put up or shut up – you can quote me on that".

The second boat is "Quicksilver", a British boat in which, apparently, Bluebird designer Ken Norris had an input. Warby said: "I still can't believe the British are still hell-bent on trying to make the reverse three-pointer work. Cobb and Taylor died trying......It almost makes me believe that there was no boat racer involved in the design, otherwise they would have known of the practical problems that occur. This concept does work well as a model and always looks good in a wind tunnel, but when it comes to making it work full-size on water, some poor driver is in for a rude shock". (Warby had always said he would rather drive a jet boat designed by a boat racer than a jet boat designed by an aerodynamicist). In any case, there had been little publicity about the Quicksilver project.

There was a third boat christened "Miss Scandinavia", and while obviously a project of the chillier top of Europe, little was known of it in 2003 except a spectacular piece of artwork. Of this, Warby's web site says: "If this boat ever gets built, it is Ken's belief that the boat will lift-off. Cat-style hull traps too much air". And he adds: "So far there is a lot of talk out there. So let's see them put their throttle foot where their mouth is".

Aussie Spirit was finally unveiled in Australia at the National Maritime Museum in Darling Harbour, where his first boat hangs high for the wonder of those under 20 who have never heard of him. But that year was the start of a bitter drought in Australia that would last through 2007 and into 2008. Blowering and Eildon were drying up fast, and with it went the length Warby would need for another attempt.

But still he didn't give up. Still firmly buttoned into his past, still reluctant to let go of Slim Dusty and Blowering and his image as the rough and struggling Aussie battler, he wetted the new boat in Australian water for the first time, on December 19, 2004, in the Manning River in Taree where he had first seriously run his record-breaker. Then on January 22, 2005, he wound up the boat there again, but given the length and width limits of the river he didn't release any speed figures. The same applied with a final

Taree run for Aussie Spirit the following June. On April 23 his father Neville died. Warby ran his new boat, by then carrying AMF sponsorship, for the last time in the US on October 16, 2007. On November 20 he announced his retirement. Typically, it was the 30th anniversary of his last – still standing – record run.

By then his great friends and record attempt controllers, Tom Fink and Bob Apathy, had also died. There were really no more repeats to be run.

His Way

Warby was back at Coniston in the Lakes district of Cumbria, UK, on October 20, 2007, just four days after he ran Aussie Spirit for the last time, in an exhibition with the AMF Off-Shore Racing Team – of which he became a patron, even being given its annual award in 2008 of "King Of Mardi Gras". He was guest speaker at a dinner in his honour at Church House Inn, Torver, using a whiteboard to sketch boat designs, he illustrated the reasons Campbell and Taylor had crashed and died.

Campbell's memory was still there to haunt him. His Bluebird K7 – and his headless body - were raised from Coniston in 2001, 34 years after the lapis-coloured Norris Brothers-designed hydroplane flew and somersaulted at around 480 km/h. It was recovered by diver Bill Smith, who in 2008 at Tyneside started restoring it, with a new Bristol Orpheus jet engine to replace Campbell's Orpheus. Warby told the dinner he didn't think his record would be broken "in the near future". He hinted then at his retirement announcement (which came one month later), saying that record-breaking was a "young man's game" and he was now too old.

The only person ever to design, build, drive, pay for and achieve a world record in his own boat was contemptuous of those planning to attack his 30-year-old record. "These.....guys have a whole bunch of airplane and computer geeks behind them. But this is fucking dangerous, and it's a boat, not an airplane. Their chances of breaking the record are absolutely zero, and I'm booking plans for two funerals", the man who never called a spade a "digging implement" told senior boating writer Carl Hoffman.

The new teams were basing models on computerised fluid dynamics to produce a shape in exotic materials that could be thoroughly tested before the hull even got wet, incorporating on-board telemetry, stability computers to control all boat movements, and ejection cockpit module – none of which even entered Warby's thinking. Both his boats were hand-made from wood and never got within shouting distance of a computer. "Shit no!" Warby told Hoffman before his retirement. "I'm not into that stuff. I call (my way) eyeball engineering, and I could drive it in a jockstrap and sandals".

But hydro-dynamics and computers aren't the entire answer. Record boats have to be hydroplanes, meaning that as speed rises they go up "on the plane", riding only on a few square centimetres of surface. The conventional theory is that every time speed doubles the aerodynamic lift is quadrupled, so – as Warby knew very well – the whole boat is subject to baffling and contradictory compromises in drag, rudder surface, spoilers, wings and weight distribution. The boat is never stable on the water; it moves around, dancing and bouncing, leaving the water completely at times, always wanting to get the nose up and fly. Even the best aerodynamicists say it smacks of being a black art.

Warby maintained (and still does) that a boat should be designed to be most stable in a slight chop, which lessens the drag factor. Campbell always wanted the surface to be like glass; he was killed partly because of the boat's aerodynamic flaws but also because he started his return run too soon and ran into the remains of his own wash. Warby is also somewhat scornful about the role of computerised electronic controls of boat behaviour – "the computer is dealing with what's behind you, not what's in front". He also slams designs using what's called a "reverse three-pointer', such as Lee Taylor's. This involves three planing contacts – one at the bow and two behind, like a tricycle.

That, however, is the basis of the boat that for five years or more has been under design by the American Challenge Team, to be driven by a 40-year-old called Russ Wicks, dubbed "The Fastest American on Water" by his formidable PR team. They boost Wicks as the only living person to hold world speed records over 200 mph (320 km/h) on land and water. He set the world record for propellor-driven unlimited hydroplanes in "Miss Freei" at 205.494 mph (330.5 km/h) and a world stock car speed record in a NASCAR-spec Ford Taurus of 222.623 mph (358.2 km/h) on the Bonneville Salt Flats in Utah in 2006.

Wicks was a fully-sponsored motocross professional at 15, and in a bid to break into European racing went to France to train in the Winfield Racing School and drive in the Elf Formula Renault series, before moving to Super Vees and testing for an Indy car seat, without success. His web site trumpets reflects the boastful ideal of the all-American-as-hero; his MySpace page has photographs of three glamorously-cleavaged women amongst his "40 friends", lists among his music loves Smashing Pumpkins, Metallica and the Rolling Stones, and his heroes as Ayrton Senna, Nikki Lauda, Evel Knievel and Donald Campbell.

There's not a mention of Ken Warby, whose music love of Slim Dusty and his scorn for celebrity bullshit make him as different to Wicks as one could be. Of Wicks' unlimited hydroplane propeller-driven world record, Warby says: "Even a trained monkey could have broken it". There is no love lost between them: In 2004 Wicks described Warby as "a Wile E Coyote going for a ride on a fibreglass board". Warby's response: "Wicks is known in boat racing as the media whore".

Built – as Wicks says – to bring the world water speed record back to the US, the "American Challenge" is being designed and built by a formidable team of high-tech companies. Their disciplines include fluid dynamics, structures, systems simulation, materials and aerospace. With access to a wind tunnel and water tank, they claim the craft will be "constructed much like a current military fighter jet". Wicks attracted serious American media attention, initially raising seed money of $5 million, of which $1.5 million was earmarked for marketing.

The promotional model of the boat certainly looked like a fighter with tiny stubby wings. It will run a General Electric F-404 engine with a potential 12,000 pounds of thrust – more than double that for Warby's second boat. In that early form it even used the canopy and ejection system from an F16 fighter – the designers say they have drawn the boat around the cockpit first. The design includes leading-edge flaps and vertical control fins, accelerometers, gyroscopes and an onboard computer. In several interviews one or two team members have made mocking references to the lack of leading edge technology in Warby's boats. Warby just grins his craggy grin.

The second major challenge comes from Britain. Probably the project that aims 51-year-old Nigel Macknight at Warby's record some time in 2010 did seem – in mid-2009, at least - closer to reality than Wicks' vision. Macknight seems to be a re-birth of the classic Boy's Own hero model – Malcolm Campbell, his son Donald, world land speed record holder Richard Noble. Born in Northumberland but raised in Lancashire, he was inspired at age 17 by a BBC documentary on Donald Campbell and tried to get famed engineer LeoVilla - who helped design Campbell's Bluebird and was a confidant of Warby's - to help him launch a new Bluebird bid for the record, lying about his age and a so-called family fortune.

That idea went nowhere, and Macknight started writing for children's magazines, and then books, publishing the definitive work on NASA's space shuttle and writing technical manuals about aeronautics. He raced karts and Formula Ford for seven years and wrote some great accounts of flights he had done with NASA and aerobatic pilots. In 1978, after watching news reports of Warby's records, he made up his mind to start his own world record project.

He began in 1999 by quitting his job, re-mortgaging his house and selling all his memorabilia, which included an archive of Campbell's photographs and a watch presented to him by Buzz Aldrin, one of the three astronauts on the first Moon landing. He got in touch with Bluebird designer Ken Norris, long retired from designing boats at 81 but who had worked with Richard Noble on thrust 2, and convinced him to lend his name to help launch project "Quicksilver". He was criticised for seeming to use Norris' name to finance his bid, and the original boat design he showed was soon abandoned for the current iteration, moving the sponsons from the rear to alongside the front..

Macknight has 40 mainly-Brit-owned companies backing him, and has used an approach very different to that of "American Challenge". The boat will not use computerised aerodynamic override controls. Macknight has rejected that approach – which he says makes it not a boat but an aircraft skimming along the water (which fairly describes today's land speed record "cars"). Instead, Quicksilver will use four planing surfaces controlled by hydraulics through computerised load cells that are adjusted according to the boat's weight changes under pitch, roll and sponson walking. But he agrees with Warby that on the run the boat's behaviour will change so quickly that no computer can compensate fast enough, so his system will limit the number of actions to relatively major changes in surface. But it will carry 86 sensors that will record and store data to on-shore laptops during a run, which will allow him to back off if danger threatens.

It will be the largest and heaviest world record boat ever built – 11.8 metres long and 3.4 metres wide and weighing 3.5 tonnes. It will need the power from its Rolls-Royce-built Hawker Siddeley Buccaneer jet engine rated at 25,000 horsepower – about three times what Campbell had in his Bluebird. At the time of writing the design plan was to locate the engine and fuel tank midships in the square steel tube and aluminium space frame, with the cockpit in one of the two stabilising floats. Macknight will lie almost flat on his back, with one pedal for throttle and one for brake. The schedule called for the first water trials near the end of 2009, to a maximum of 160 km/h, with the window for the record attempt at Lake Coniston January-March 2012.

As more details of both challenger boats emerged, Warby remained loyal to his "eyeball engineering" – the stuff that carried him to two world records in a boat now regarded as primitive. To writer Carl Hoffman he said: "They better have some awful smart people programming those computers. When you look down that lake, you better have all your homework done, because your chances are 50-50 – and you better be in the right 50 percent. And you better be doing it for the right reasons. If I blow through the trap at 400 and nobody even knows about it, that's OK. I do it for myself, because I know I've built a better mousetrap".

Throughout this book there have been references to Warby's selfishness in his single-minded pursuit of excellence. However, implicit in his re-invention of himself as a record-breaker was the overwhelming understanding that it was not self-interest that drives him but a self-confidence that is awesome in the extreme, as well as his demonstrated ability to learn by experience, and his trust and confidence in the people around him. Essentially an unsentimental but complex man, he does not gladly tolerate fools but retains great respect for people – perhaps like himself – who have displayed their own confidence in their own knowledge and ability – their own selfishness, if you like. One suspects his motto has always been: "Don't tell me what I can't do and what can't happen – let's get on with it".

Ken Warby did what he did for Ken Warby, not for anyone else, not for his wives, his partners, his children or his sponsors. Ken Warby, he of the reputed weak heart as a boy, Ken Warby who stole pages of magazines from his local library to read up on water speed record boats, Ken Warby who built wooden boats that defied the knockers in the local boat clubs, Ken Warby who went – let us never deny nor seek to minimise this – where no man had ever gone. He scaled his personal Everest on the basis of his own clear aims, his understanding of himself, his determination……this man, regardless of what might have happened if he ever had put his second boat into the water at Blowering, near Tumut, this private lunatic on a long, dark, echoing lake, this very Australian man who loves Slim Dusty and who felt the cold dead hand of the ghost of

Donald Campbell, can never, ever, suffer that essentially Australian curse of being called a bullshit artist.

Perhaps – just perhaps – his own country that has ignored him for far too long will in time come to understand that.